Warwickshire County Council

D0334860

This item is to be returned or renewed before the
latest date above. It may be borrowed for a further
period if not in demand. **To renew your books:**

- **Phone the 24/7 Renewal Line 01926 499273 or**
- **Visit www.warwickshire.gov.uk/libraries**

Discover • Imagine • Learn • _with libraries_

Warwickshire
County Council

Working for
Warwickshire

PRAISE FOR *SIX WEEKS OF BLENHEIM SUMMER*

'One can't help feeling awe and reverence for people like this. There are enough adventures here for a lifetime, let alone six weeks.'

– Louis de Bernières

'The late Alastair Panton and his granddaughter, Victoria, have combined to produce a gripping account of the traumatic early days of World War Two. *Six Weeks of Blenheim Summer* tells an amazing story of bravery and courage in the air and on the ground. I commend it as a book that will appeal equally to the military historian and the general reader alike.'

– General the Lord Dannatt GCB CBE MC DL, former head of the British Army

'This story grips you by the lapels and sometimes by the throat, and all who love tales of war will devour every page; but I'd especially recommend it to non-WW2-addicts, for it's really a story of failure, reminding us that courage and skill don't always win the day, but are to be valued for themselves.'

– Matthew Parris, *Times* columnist

'As a former member of the Royal Air Force I read this book with immense anticipation. These men were pushed far beyond limits; to be shot down again and again and to keep going is beyond words. Alastair Panton's courage, determination and professionalism in terrible circumstances are astounding. It is because of men like Alastair that I'm so proud to have been part of the RAF.'

– Duncan Slater, first double amputee to reach the South Pole, former sergeant and RAF veteran

'I was riveted by this story set during the grim days of the German *Blitzkrieg* through France in 1940. Alastair Panton's tale of how he and his RAF crews contributed to the fight against the advancing Nazis is utterly enthralling. His concern for his brother, still fighting with the 51st Highland Division weeks after Dunkirk, is a very moving aspect of the book. Highly recommended.'

– Brigadier Hugh Monro CBE, former Highland soldier and Chief Inspector of Prisons for Scotland

SIX WEEKS OF
BLENHEIM SUMMER

SIX WEEKS OF
BLENHEIM SUMMER

AN RAF OFFICER'S
MEMOIR OF THE
BATTLE OF FRANCE 1940

ALASTAIR PANTON AND
VICTORIA PANTON BACON

Biteback Publishing

First published in Great Britain in 2014 by
Biteback Publishing
Westminster Tower
3 Albert Embankment
London SE1 7SP

ISBN 978-1-84954-668-3

10 9 8 7 6 5 4 3 2 1

A CIP catalogue record for this book is available from the British Library.

Set in Caslon by 525 Graphic Design
Printed and bound in Great Britain by
CPI Group (UK) Ltd, Croydon CR0 4YY

MIX
Paper from
responsible sources
FSC® C020471

CONTENTS

Alastair Panton was one of the heroes in France during the dark days of 1940 when the Allies looked as though they were losing the war. In the summer of 1940, the Germans swept into Belgium and France crushing the Allies before them. Panton has left us a remarkable memoir which is in no way boastful but relates what those confronting the Germans felt at the time.

It seems extraordinary today that so much happened in the six weeks Panton writes about. He was shot down three times, wounded, and saw his comrades killed, sometimes dying in agony. He and his fellow pilots flew day after day, sometimes more than once, always knowing that death was ever present. They had to be continuously courageous and overcome the stress and strain with which all pilots had to contend. Alastair Panton was a leader who captained a Bristol Blenheim Mark IV throughout those six weeks and became fond of, even dependent on, his plane. He knew how reliable it was, its strengths and weaknesses, and how his crew could use it to reconnoitre and influence the battlefield and save lives. It saved his life on numerous occasions.

Panton was eventually captured by the Germans and spent the rest of the war as a prisoner. I know of few other memoirs which capture the atmosphere of war in the air better than *Six Weeks of Blenheim Summer*. One never feels that the author got satisfaction from what he did. So many of his friends and comrades died and he felt particularly strongly about those who were close to him and for whom he was responsible. He always felt that his six weeks of Blenheim summer were a failure. His fascinating account deserves to be widely read. It is beautifully written and we owe much to Panton's granddaughter, Victoria Panton Bacon, who edits and introduces it. It is a fitting tribute to a sensitive, gallant and great Englishman.

Alastair Panton sitting on the body of a Bristol Blenheim,
shortly after he was awarded the Distinguished Flying Cross
for gallantry in March 1940.

Photograph printed with permission of the Imperial War Museum.

INTRODUCTION BY
VICTORIA PANTON BACON

Written by my grandfather, Alastair Dyson Panton, *Six Weeks of Blenheim Summer* is a dramatic account of flying Bristol Blenheims as an RAF reconnaissance pilot in France and the Low Countries during the summer of 1940. I found the memoir in an old brown envelope, nestled in a box among some of my father's wartime model aeroplanes, stored in his garage, shortly after he died in August 2012. There is much pain and sadness in *Blenheim Summer,* which I think is why my father hid it away. However, after reading it I felt compelled to take it further, both to remember Alastair, and as a mark of gratitude to the many brave and courageous men who served with him. I think Alastair would have wanted those who died to be remembered.

The memoir starts on 11 May 1940, and takes

the reader through the following six weeks, a part of World War Two now known to history as the Battle of France. The battle actually started one day before, when Germany began its invasions into the Netherlands and Belgium. Grandfather's six weeks finish on 18 June, a few days before the battle ended with the successful occupation of France by Germany.

In those six weeks, Alastair was shot down three times. First, after being shot at, he crash-landed his burning aircraft in enemy territory and, while evading capture, brought his injured crew back to Allied lines (only to learn of the rapidly worsening military situation). Second, when an unexploded shell penetrated his cockpit and destroyed his steering column, leaving him no option but to coax his Blenheim back to English airspace and bale out of his burning aircraft (only to find his parachute was on fire). Third, while reluctantly following orders to fly low over the Dunkirk beaches in order to encourage the retreating British soldiers, his Blenheim was shot down by friendly fire. He was forced to crash-land on the beach, jump from his port wing and race away from the exploding remains of his aircraft (finding himself next to a surprised Roman Catholic padre who, moments earlier, had been celebrating Mass on the seashore), before joining the miraculous exodus from Dunkirk by boat.

However, the *Boys' Own* quality of some of his deeds cannot hide the dreadful and painful reality. Only the day before he departed from Nantes, the troopship *Lancastria*, crammed with RAF troops as well as civilian women and children, had been bombed and sunk by German aircraft near the port of St Nazaire some 40 miles away. Over 3,000 lives were lost, including members of Alastair's unit who were also returning to England.

The memoir brings to life the fear, loneliness, physical pain and terrible sadness that Alastair, and so many of his comrades, came to live with. It also draws on the bravery, camaraderie and humanity that made these unpredictable days more bearable. It is the story of a pilot and his plane. He captained a Bristol Blenheim throughout this time, sometimes taking to the skies as many as five times a day. He came to see the Blenheim as his hero – it was the vehicle from which he and his crew were able to spot enemy tanks and subsequently save lives. As Alastair writes: 'The affection and trust I had quickly developed for my

Blenheim under normal conditions became wondering admiration as it triumphed over shocking abuse.' Even in the terrifying adversity, Alastair describes how his 'poor, gallant, blazing Blenheim' allowed him to make a safe crash-landing and thus dramatically rescue his two crew members.

Alastair writes poignantly in his own introduction that *Blenheim Summer* is a story of failure. This early part of the Second World War was, indeed, a period of crippling and painful defeat for the Allies. However, it was also a key turning point in military history: the scale of loss in May 1940 alone led Prime Minister Winston Churchill to command a speedy withdrawal of British troops from France at the end of that month, an operation known now as the Evacuation of Dunkirk. The success of this operation, in which Alastair played a part, enabled Britain to rebuild its defences and, some years later, to declare victory.

A month after the events he describes in his book, Alastair was shot down a fourth time, captured, and made a prisoner of war. This time his gunner was engulfed in fire and there was nothing Alastair could do. I know he never forgot the screams he heard that day and, consequently, I think he attached a feeling of failure to himself, as well as to what was going on around him. Alastair was certainly not a failure, but I think he was so traumatised by the events he describes in his book that feelings of pride would have been obliterated. While Alastair survived, many did not. Of the twenty-two members in his unit, Alastair was one of only three who lived to see the end of the war. That guilt, and the grief of so much loss, never left him.

Grandfather undoubtedly played a vital role within the British Expeditionary Force (BEF) during the Battle of France, and his story is one of extraordinary courage, bravery and survival. However, I would be doing him a disservice if any reader should think I have sought publication of his memoir in order to present him as hero, with an audacity that surpassed his comrades; he was among hundreds of equally heroic servicemen, coming under fire, many of whom suffered life-threatening injuries, amputated limbs or death. Therefore, my grandfather's fortitude was not unique; but maybe the fact he has told his story in this way is, and in doing so he is describing a period of the Second World War that has not been so colourfully portrayed before.

I should point out that *Blenheim Summer* records my grandfather's recollections of this time, written up some forty years after he was repatriated to England. I have checked the facts as much as possible, and much of this checking has confirmed the sharpness of memory he refers to in his own introduction. However, *Blenheim Summer* is his story; what has been inserted or omitted I cannot explain. I believe he made the decision to write up his memories in this way in order to keep this period of history alive, not for it to be used as an accurate historical record. Now his story is in print I hope the words will do for many what they have done for me – bring home, intensely, the sacrifice made by so many brave men like Alastair, and the gratitude we continue to owe them.

Alastair was awarded the Distinguished Flying Cross for gallantry before the start of the campaign in 1940. Fergus, Alastair's youngest brother, wrote about how proud he was of Alastair for receiving this award, which, according to Fergus, was for perilous reconnaissance flights taking aerial photographs in 'ancient slow machines' (Lysanders). Alastair's service was further recognised with an OBE in 1950 and a CB in 1969. By the time he retired in 1971, Air Commodore Alastair Dyson Panton was Provost Marshal of the Royal Air Force and Head of RAF Security. He died in December 2002 aged eighty-six.

Blenheim Summer is dedicated, on my grandfather's behalf, to his family: surviving sons Andrew and David, their wives Bridget and Sheelagh, his grandchildren Richard, Henry, Sarah, Giles, Catriona, Neil, Alex and Antonia, and his great-grandchildren Barnaby, Sapphire, Pollyanna, Rollo, Ranulph, Hector and Wilbur. Granny Isabel, Alastair's wife, who died in 2000, also deserves a special mention, as does Elizabeth, my mother, who died in 2007.

Finally, *Blenheim Summer* is dedicated to my father, Stephen, Alastair's eldest son. My father was not a pilot but he shared his father's love of flight, and there was very little he did not know about wartime aeroplanes. By the time he died he had made more than one thousand model aircraft. His earliest was a Supermarine Spitfire Mark IX, the latest was an EE Canberra PR9, and in between there were Fokker Triplanes, Sopwith Camels, Hawker Typhoons,

Hawker Siddeley Vulcans, de Havilland Mosquitos, Messerschmitts, Fairey Swordfish and, of course, a collection of lovingly crafted Bristol Blenheims.

If I hadn't discovered the transcript of *Blenheim Summer* in my father's dusty garage it might never have come to light.

Victoria Panton Bacon
May 2014

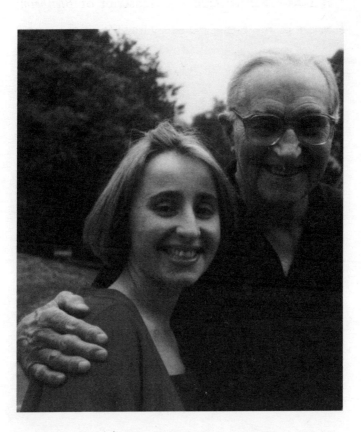

Victoria with her Grandfather, Alastair Panton, circa 1995.

Family photograph taken by Victoria's mother, Elizabeth.

PROLOGUE

May and June 1940 were two of the most devast-ating months of the Second World War for the Allies. France surrendered to Germany on 22 June, following the capitulation of the Netherlands and Belgium the previous month. In these two months alone, around 85,000 French servicemen were killed and 120,000 wounded. Almost 68,000 British servicemen lost their lives, were wounded or were captured and taken as prisoners of war.

By the end of May 1940 Winston Churchill, who had succeeded Neville Chamberlain as Minister of Defence on 10 May, ordered the Evacuation of Dunkirk, rescuing thousands of British men as the German armies closed in.

Six Weeks of Blenheim Summer illuminates the events of the Battle of France through the eyes of my grandfather, who at the time was a young flying officer in the RAF. This battle was one of a number of battles throughout World War Two, each of which played their part in determining the eventual outcome. This prologue attempts to put this part of the war into historical context, and I hope it will broaden the reader's understanding of my grandfather Alastair Panton's story.

Alastair begins his memoir on 11 May 1940, the day after the Battle of France began. The day before, when the German incursions into the Netherlands and Belgium finally began, they were not unexpected. Such attacks had been anticipated immediately after Neville Chamberlain announced on 3 September 1939 that Britain was officially at war with Germany. Mobilisation of the British Expeditionary Force (BEF), comprising the army, navy and air force, had begun in Britain as soon as war was declared. Fortunately, thousands of these active young men had heeded the Secretary of State for War Alfred Duff Cooper's advice to join the military services during the profound economic depression of the 1930s. Men from all economic and social classes flourished, learning new skills and trades in the navy, army and air force. For the first time, they had a sense of individual achievement and their families prospered, rather than waiting for unemployment benefit. The BEF incorporated many of these servicemen, now in the regular British Army or Territorial Army. Therefore, troops were able to assemble quickly after the declaration, and were deployed to Europe to take up strategic positions along the Franco-Belgian border, in preparation for an invasion.

Over the next few months, troops, materiel and vehicles continued to arrive in France and Belgium and, by 13 March 1940, the BEF had doubled in size to 316,000 men. However, the BEF and its Allies were kept waiting, in a period which became known as the 'Phoney War' as nothing of any real consequence occurred, save for a few minor clashes and incursions on the ground and in the air. Yet when the war ceased to be phoney and reality set in, it did so with the Germans deploying the crippling lightning war techniques known as *Blitzkrieg*. This strategy combined assault by land and by air to ensure rapid progress – essentially, air raids with parachute drops followed by attacks from tanks and troops on the ground. The *Blitzkrieg* by the Germans capitalised on surprise penetrations and their opponents' inability to react swiftly. It was devastatingly effective: by 12 May, Rotterdam in the Netherlands was surrounded and Germany had captured strategic bridges and seized airfields near The Hague. The Dutch relented and by 15 May their surrender was complete. Belgium also proved to be not much more than a sitting duck and by 28 May it too had fallen into German hands.

Early on in the campaign, using the *Blitzkrieg* technique, Germany had powered its way into France through the Ardennes Forest. This is an enormous region of extensive woodland, hills and rough terrain in north-east France, which also extends into Belgium, Luxembourg and Germany. The success of the German approach through this area took the French by surprise, as it had not occurred to them that mechanised forces would be able to function in such difficult terrain.

However, it was to the south of this region at Sedan, 6 miles from the Belgian border, where hundreds of German tanks were able to penetrate into France, crossing the River Meuse, which allowed them to bypass the French fortification system (the infamous Maginot Line). Ineffective Allied counter-attacks did not stop the German mechanised forces, enabling them to entrap the British and French, who were unable to respond in strength to German attacks in the north. This underestimation of German strength and mobility proved to be disastrous. Lord Gort, commander of the BEF and working to a 1914–18 timetable, expected that he would have two or three weeks to prepare for the Germans to travel 65 miles. The Germans would actually arrive in four days!

On 5 June, the second act of the Battle of France began, with a major offensive from Germany which saw heavy fighting in the area of the Somme. This fight began with the Germans invading the region to the south of this important river. The French put up a considerable defence and the German losses were substantial, in spite of their enormous numerical superiority. Once again, the German army relied on the Luftwaffe to help, by silencing French guns and enabling German infantry and tanks to move forward. Three days later, the French had been overwhelmed and began withdrawing their troops from the area. The situation for France worsened progressively. On 10 June, the Italian dictator Mussolini joined forces with Germany, declaring war on Britain and

France. On 11 June, the Germans launched a major offensive on the French capital, Paris, one day after it had been declared an 'open city'. With the French line of resistance broken in several places around Paris, the French government was forced to flee to Bordeaux.

France, by now, had become a politically divided country. On 16 June, its then Prime Minister, Paul Reynaud, resigned and was replaced by Marshal Philippe Pétain. The following day, Pétain appealed to the French troops to stop fighting, and addressed the French citizens on the radio, announcing that he would seek an armistice with Germany. Spasmodic skirmishes continued for a few days but, on 22 June, France surrendered. Hitler insisted on signing the document of capitulation at Compiègne Forest, in the same railway carriage that was used for the 1918 Armistice that had ultimately ended the First World War. The humiliation of France continued with its division. Pétain's control was limited to the south, his capital at Vichy in central France. The Germans, in return, occupied northern France and France's entire Atlantic coastline down to the border with Spain.

That said, the Germans did not have everything their way during the summer of 1940. The French put up a courageous fight throughout, including against the enemy encircling Dunkirk at the end of May, when more than a third of a million Allied troops were successfully transported out of the war-torn area in an operation known now as the Evacuation of Dunkirk. Codenamed Operation Dynamo, this evacuation of troops began on 27 May 1940 and was completed by 4 June.

It could have been one of the worst disasters in military history: still trapped by the Germans, and depleted of military resources by the *Blitzkrieg*, the BEF was essentially at the mercy of the German Luftwaffe, which did its best to prevent the seaborne evacuation. However, the Germans did not take into account the negative effect that sand on the beaches would have on its bombs, or of the unstinting support from many French and Belgian civilians who came to the aid of British troops.

Vice Admiral Bertram Ramsay masterminded the hastily prepared operation on the British side: he mobilised an assortment of vessels, including passenger-ferry steamers, Thames barges and tugs, to take the beleaguered servicemen back home. The Dutch, too, came to the assistance of the BEF, providing around forty passenger

ships from the Royal Navy. However, it was soon realised that many more, shallower craft were required
than the navy could supply to ferry personnel from
the beaches out to these larger craft waiting off shore.
Ramsay made an emergency call on the radio for
additional help from private boat owners throughout
Britain; they responded admirably.

On the first full day of the evacuation, 7,669 men
had been evacuated. By the ninth day, a total of 338,226
servicemen had been returned to England, in a fleet of
over 800 boats, in which nearly 400 small craft with
civilian seafarers had voluntarily and enthusiastically
taken part.

The departure of troops from this small harbour
town in northern France was ordered by the British
Prime Minister, Winston Churchill, and its 'success'
proved to be an important turning point in Second
World War history, not least of all because it gave
Britain a basis on which to rebuild its defences, and
was a key factor in persuading the United States (then
neutral) to support the Allies. In a speech to the House
of Commons, Winston Churchill said: 'The tale of the
Dunkirk beaches will shine in whatever records are
preserved of our affairs', but warned that 'we must be

very careful not to assign to this deliverance the attributes of a victory. Wars are not won by evacuations.'

Grandfather's role during the Battle of France
was to pilot the long-nose Mark IV version of the
Bristol Blenheim aeroplane. With his crew of two,
they flew on reconnaissance operations, establishing
the whereabouts of the enemy, and reported their
discoveries back to base and down the chain of
command. The Blenheim was a British light bomber
aircraft, designed and built by the Bristol Aeroplane
Company. It first took to the skies in 1935 and was
flown extensively in the early days of the Second World
War. With its metal fuselage, armour plate and defensive guns, the Blenheim proved its worth against most
biplane fighters in the late 1930s and early 1940s.
But, as the war progressed and the Luftwaffe stepped
up its aggression, the more powerful, single-engine
Messerschmitt 109 fighters out-performed the obsol-
ete, lightly armed RAF Bristol Blenheim bombers
and, by 1944, a process of phasing out the remaining
Blenheims had virtually been completed.

Grandfather and his crewmen, Sergeant Alan E. Farrow, Sergeant Leslie H. Stride, Sergeant William A. Christie and AC2 R. Bence, were all members of 53 Squadron of the Royal Air Force, whose motto was 'United in Effort'. Early in 1939, 53 Squadron's role was to be a specialist reconnaissance and surveyor unit with a tactical element. After war was announced, the squadron left Odiham in Hampshire, as part of the air component of the BEF in France, on survey misisons over the BEF area.

The British air forces in France consisted of two separate formations. The air component of the BEF went to France to support the British and French armies. Bomber Command formed the Advanced Air Striking Forces (AASF). An agreement with the French government and Military Staff in the late 1930s meant that, in the event of war, a highly mobile, light RAF bomber force could move to designated forward-operating bases on French soil around Rheims to bomb Germany should the political decision to do so be taken. The AASF consisted of eight squadrons of Fairey Battles, two squadrons with Bristol Blenheim light bombers, and two squadrons of Hawker Hurricane fighters. An additional five Westland Lysander squadrons were added to this component under the overall command of Air Vice Marshal Arthur 'Ugly' Barratt before the opening shots were fired in anger.

When the intense bombing of Belgium and the Netherlands began on 10 May 1940, 53 Squadron was one of the first squadrons to be thrown immediately into battle to survey the region, scrambling seven aircraft to carry out the reconnaissance. These included the Blenheim Grandfather flew, L9459 PZ-G, which, after several successful flights, was attacked and crash-landed.

53 Squadron continued this forward aerial reconnaissance role by day and flew recces of German cities (Hanover, Minden, Hamm, Bremen, Osnabrück and Münster) by night. But the night missions did not spare the squadron from suffering heavy casualties: losses ran to about two aircraft per day.

The fighting in France in the summer of 1940 cost the RAF a total of 1,029 aircraft and over 1,500 of its personnel. On 14 May alone, the RAF lost thirty-nine out of seventy-one aircraft – the highest concentration of losses of men and aircraft in a single operation of that size it has ever sustained. When 'Ugly' Barratt heard of the toll he hung a 'Do Not Disturb' sign on his door and wept.

Six Weeks of Blenheim Summer is the written memoir of Alastair Panton's own recollections of this battle, but the experiences he has described were, of course, shared by so many. By learning about a little of what Alastair experienced, we can perhaps appreciate the horror that so many went through, as the German *Blitzkrieg* cut a swathe through Europe with such devastating consequences.

Editor's note: The names of Alastair's crew members are correct, other names may not be.

Map taken from RAF Narrative 21 showing the campaign in
France and the low countries 1939–1940, produced by the Air
Historical Branch.

Map kindly sourced and supplied by the Research Department at RAF Hendon.

CHAPTER 1

ALASTAIR'S INTRODUCTION

In the course of a conversation my son David and I had about some of my short stories, he asked me if I had ever thought of writing about being in France in 1940. Remarks of mine in past years about my experiences in a country that was collapsing around me had always stirred his interest. Almost all the writings on the war which he had read had had successful endings, but he had often thought that a scenario of failure would read very differently. This is a story of failure.

I have divided it into three parts: before, during and after the Dunkirk evacuation. In the first and third parts, circumstances gave me a lone hand to play. I have called the second part 'Dunkirk Interlude' because it is truly an interlude in my story. It differs in two ways from the other two parts: firstly, the Dunkirk evacuation of the British Expeditionary Force ended successfully, even if failure caused it to happen; and secondly, I was not on my own, but playing my part in the operational tasks given to 53 Squadron.

Although my six weeks are of a summer more than forty years ago, I lived those six weeks very intensely, and my memories are very sharp. The events happened as I have described them. As I write, I can clearly recall the stinging heat of a burning Blenheim; smells, tastes, expressions, sounds of voices, the difficulties of some landings, sights, and, most of all, fear gripping deep in me. To keep my story lively I have recorded conversations as direct speech. I cannot, of course, after so long a period, remember the actual words, although in some instances I certainly can. The words do, however, convey the sense and atmosphere as closely as I can make them.

I hope David and the rest of my family find the record interesting. The further you are removed from the war, the harder you will find it to accept that these things actually happened to the ageing person my grandchildren know. If you do feel that, I shall understand. In mind and body I am now very different, but one thing is the same: my memory. If I could meet my

23-year-old self, I think we would agree that it is only a coincidence that the same memory occupies such a different mind and body.

I said this is a story of failure, but I have to make one resounding exception: the part played throughout the flying sequences by my Bristol Blenheim Mark IV with its Bristol Mercury engines.

Under normal conditions of operation and maintenance, I found my Blenheim easy and reliable to fly. As a pilot of 53 Squadron my primary role was to take overlapping vertical photographs for map correction purposes. This required accurate flying, with instruments, for long periods. As far as I remember, I had to maintain an accuracy of plus or minus 50 feet in height and plus or minus 2 degrees of heading at a, near as possible, constant air-speed. My Blenheim met these requirements admirably as a platform for the cameras. At the same time, meeting them made it an uncomfortably easy target for enemy fighters.

The affection and trust I had quickly developed for my Blenheim under normal conditions became wondering admiration as it triumphed over shocking abuse during the six-week campaign of my story. At times we operated with no maintenance crews; the robustness of the airframe was continuously tested by being dumped hurriedly down onto short, rough landing spaces, and the Mercury engines stood up well to being driven at times far beyond the safety limits of boost and revolutions. I must confess to having one constantly recurring wish: that my Blenheim would go 100mph faster, but, at that stage of aeronautical development, that was asking for the moon, as I well knew.

CHAPTER 2

BELGIUM AND
PAS-DE-CALAIS

11 May 1940 – 04.30

In the months before May 1940 my crew and I had flown three uneventful, but successful, daylight reconnaissance sorties over the heavily defended Ruhr region in West Germany. Surviving these flights and the long hours we had spent practising our survey photography had filled us with confidence. However, as the sun rose in the sky over our small airfield in Poix, near Amiens, I could not help but be filled with apprehension because the day before three out of six aircraft in our flight, all engaged on the same photographic tasks as ourselves, had not returned.

Our crew, Christie, Bence and myself, had been flying together for over a year and a half. They had come to me from their training schools when 53 Squadron received its Mark IV Blenheims. We had worked hard at perfecting the technique needed for survey photography, our primary role. My job was to keep our Blenheim at the required height, speed and heading by keeping my eyes steadfastly on the instrument panel, while Christie concentrated on passing me the small alterations needed to keep us on the right heading. This he did by constantly cross-referring between the line on his map and his Aldiss sight, a prismatic instrument mounted vertically in the floor of the cockpit. The Aldiss sight was used in Coastal Command rear facing to calculate drift; we turned ours round forward facing to show us where we were heading. While Christie and I concentrated on our instruments, Bence's part was to keep quartering the sky from his gun turret, looking out for other aircraft, particularly enemy ones.

Occasionally, as a break, we had carried out a little practice bombing in case it was required of us, and Bence fired his guns at air and ground targets when we could arrange them. He was eighteen and only just old enough to be allowed overseas. Christie was the old man of the crew at twenty-eight, and I was almost exactly half-way between them.

The British Expeditionary Force had begun its

advance into Belgium to dig in along a planned line early in the morning the previous day – 10 May 1940. Our task, and that of the other five crews in our flight, was to carry out a photographic survey of the area in front of that line, which in theory was to hold the advancing Germans. Our photographs would be used to make accurate maps for the direction of artillery fire. Although our plans for the day's flying were complete, we had to wait for 'first photographic light'; before this time the shadows cast by the newly risen sun made the photographs unacceptable to the map makers. We planned our take-off time so that we could start photographing on arrival in our target area.

I was fortunate with my crew; we had bonded well as a team and we trusted each other. However, that morning, as we sat next to our Blenheim waiting for the sun to dictate when we should take to the sky, I was acutely aware of the reality of war. Germany had finally unleashed her aggression and made her intentions clear. I knew I had to do my utmost to keep a clear head at all times for Christie and Bence, but also for my squadron and my country. I was determined to return with the photographic information needed to limit the advance of the enemy.

53 Squadron had been at Poix and billeted in the village since October of the year before, 1939. Although the squadron strength had just about doubled the population, and added greatly to their income, the villagers had kept aloof. They tolerated us, but took no personal interest in our activities. Indeed, this disinterest seemed to apply to the war in general.

A notable exception was Madame Foullens, the old lady in whose cottage I was billeted. That morning and the morning before, sensing an abnormal amount of early activity, she had seen me off, standing in her bedroom doorway in an enormous, tent-like flannel night-dress, calling to me as I passed *'Bonne chance, bonne chance, mon petit! Crackez les Boches! Crackez les Boches!'* I had given up trying to explain to her why I spent my flying hours taking photographs instead of killing Germans.

In the Franco-Prussian War, as a young girl, she had been evacuated from her home. She had remained on her husband's farm in German-occupied France in 1914, becoming a war-widow, and was now still full of hostility. In retrospect I was to realise the significance of her '*Crackez les Boches.*' She was one of the very few of her countrymen to give me any support and encouragement.

She and I were great friends, and had been from my arrival at her cottage. About twice a month she would have friends in for an evening's chat with cakes and coffee, and was always anxious that I would be in from our mess, where I had all my meals, in time to join her and her friends for a cognac. Having her own Briton made her one up on them. At first, my schoolboy French gave the ladies much mirth and entertainment. Then, as I became more fluent and idiomatic, they took equally amused pleasure in the improvement, for which they took full credit.

Dear Madame Foullens! The first evening I went to her cottage it was after night-fall. She unlocked the front door, and I had to wait while she locked herself into her bedroom. After the second evening I had my own front door key, and her bedroom door would be left ajar. If she was still awake, she would light her candle and call me in for a chat. I would find her perched on her enormous feather mattress, her little, round, red face smiling and her eyes bright under the fringe of her night-cap.

Our very easy relations dated from my third early morning with her. The loo was a wooden seat over a deep pit across the yard where hens were active. By the back door stood her clogs into which she changed from her house-slippers whenever she went into the yard. That morning I did not grasp the significance of the slippers by the door and the absence of the clogs. I hurried across to the loo, which lacked any door, to come to an abrupt stop in ghastly embarrassment by finding Madame Foullens enthroned. I staggered back out of sight, blushing, muttering something about '*mille pardons*', but Madame roared with laughter and told me to stay there and have a chat with her. This we did, interrupted by an occasional grunt from her, until she said '*Et maintenant, mon brave, j'ai fini*', reaching out for the cut-up sheets of newspaper. I withdrew thankfully out of earshot, and never ventured out of the back door again unless the clogs gave me an all-clear.

In those months before the Germans invaded the Low Countries, we worked more or less normal working hours with weekends off and leave periods. We missed the comparative luxury of Odiham, our last peace-time station, and I missed my own car, but otherwise life was pleasant enough. The food in some of the restaurants in Amiens was superb, and in those days a pound went a long way. I had two memorable trips to Paris to play rugby for the Royal Air Force. On one of these trips I was walking down the Champs Élysées on a brilliant April Sunday morning in my freshly cleaned and pressed uniform with my new DFC ribbon bright under my pilot's wings. The pavement cafes were crowded, and I was admiring the colourful dresses of the ladies and their chic hats. I shall always remember hearing one of these ladies saying to the two girls at her table '*Voyez! Aviateur Anglais! Formidable!*'

As we sat on the grass at Poix, on 11 May 1940, Paris could have been a decade, not three weeks, away.

⁂

The day before we had flown for over eleven hours, more than twice as much as I had ever flown in one day before, in brilliant weather with an extraordinary feeling of being in an unreal vacuum. No one on either side had taken any notice of us all day. At 17,000 feet we had flown solidly up and down over our target area taking our reels of overlapping photographs. We had seen many, many more aircraft than we had ever seen at one time before; formations of Luftwaffe aircraft, mostly bombers hitting some fighters which had passed over us at various heights and in various directions. Everywhere the sky had been filled with condensation trails, at that time an inexplicable phenomenon to us, which only added to the feeling of unreality.

⁂

On this second day, we duly took off from Poix and returned five hours later, as programmed and as we fully expected, to hand in our exposed reels of film, to refuel, eat, and take on fresh film. Another aircraft from our flight was overdue.

On being asked by army intelligence officers, newly arrived and frantically busy strangers, if we had anything to report, Sergeant Christie and I did say that we wondered what use much of our film would be because, from what we could see, the Germans had already penetrated much more deeply than expected. Perhaps, we suggested, we should be switched to some other area, or, shades of Madame Foullens, to some other task such as bombing. Our interrogators were clearly nonplussed.

Some telephone reference was made to some authority not revealed to us, and we were brusquely told to carry on as directed. This we did, and three hours later our vacuum of isolation was shattered, along with our confidence. We were attacked by six German fighters, Messerschmitt (ME) 109s.

11 May 1940 – 14.15

For perhaps a minute and a half, diving and twisting through space which seemed to be filled with bullets rather than air, we fought them until a burst shattered my instrument panel and my starboard engine exploded into flame. At the same time a scream of agony and 'They've got me! They've got me!' came from Bence into my earphones. As Christie turned towards me, blood burst across his forehead and he slumped over the maps on his slender navigator's table. By this time the ground was coming up fast towards me. I still had some control, but there was little I could do except thrust my poor, gallant, blazing Blenheim through the tops of some trees and a bunch of electric cables beyond them onto a large meadow which providentially appeared before me. I hauled Christie by his parachute harness half out of the cockpit hatch when he came to enough to clamber out on his own. On the ground I dragged him clear of the mass of flame and thick, black smoke, and went back to see if I could do anything for Bence. To my amazement I saw his head appear momentarily from his opened gun turret, before he slumped back into a sudden burst of smoke and flame. This cleared as I jumped onto the fuselage enough for me to see him lying inert. I grabbed his harness and hauled him out.

Until he screamed, I thought he was dead; certainly his left thigh was a horrible mess. As I dragged him to where Christie lay, the ME 109s dived down, one after the other, their bullets stuttering across the ground around us, before they wheeled exultantly away. Petrol and ammunition from the Blenheim were exploding viciously, and a bundle of burning film flew derisively past me. With an uncomfortable feeling that German soldiers might appear at any moment, I dragged the two sergeants, both now unconscious, to a thick hedge and pushed them under it.

I left them to look for help. Being shot down,

although it then seemed a shattering personal experience, was to become a commonplace which many others, including myself, would experience all over the world during the next five years.

What followed was something I was to share with Christie and Bence only and only partly with them at that; they were unconscious for much of the time.

A country road bordered the field, and, seeing the roof of a large house some 300 yards away through some trees, I set off along this road towards the house. I came to a gate opening onto a drive, and, as I walked up the drive, the crackling of the dying pyre of my Blenheim was the only sound. Next to the house was a two-car garage in one side of which was a small Renault saloon. The first door of the house was half-open and, when my pull on the wrought-iron handle brought no response, I entered.

A door on the left of the hall inside the front door led to a dining room, and there, on a beautifully appointed table with cut glass, silver cutlery and damask linen, lunch for four had obviously just begun. A white wine filled, or partially filled, the glasses, and on the plates lay some pieces of fried fish. Dropped napkins and fish knives and forks showed a hurried departure. At one place a fish lay open on the plate with the backbone removed. Thirsty and hungry, I emptied a glass of wine, seized the fish by the tail, put back my head and lowered the fish into my mouth, chomping it down. As I straightened up, I caught a glimpse in a mirror of what I thought was someone behind me, and spun round startled.

No one was there. I looked back in the mirror and found that I had been startled by the reflection of my own face; my eyes and ears had been protected by my goggles and helmet, but the rest of my face was black with smoke and heavily blistered. 'God!' I thought. 'What a mess! If I come on someone in the house suddenly, I'll scare them rigid!'

Back in the hall, I called out 'Hullo! Hullo!' without response. Thinking of Christie's head and Bence's thigh, I ran upstairs into a bedroom. Although there were many signs of hurried packing, the two beds had been made. I ripped the sheets off them and ran with them back down the stairs. In the dining room I slugged back two more glasses of wine, grabbed two flagons of wine and water off the side board, and started through the front door down the drive. Then I stopped, remembering the Renault; as the occupants of the house had probably gone off in the larger of their two cars, perhaps the Renault was going spare. I'd have it.

Thankfully, the ignition key was in the lock and the Renault was full of petrol. With the bed-sheets piled on the seat beside me, the two flagons of wine and water on the floor, my flying boots clumsy on the pedals, and at the wheel of a left-hand-drive car for the first time, I was soon back in the field, bumping across the grass to where I had left Christie and Bence under the hedge.

Christie had come to, but only just. He looked blankly at the car and muttered something about it being a 'verra good idea, sir'. I gave him a drink of wine and water, tore a strip off one of the sheets, and wrapped it round his forehead, which had almost stopped bleeding. Bence was still unconscious. His left thigh was a horrible pulpy mess, but as far as I could see he was not wounded anywhere else. I wound more strips of sheet round his thigh, making it as solid as I could. The drink had done Christie good, because he was able to follow my slow clear instructions to help me pull the inert Bence into the Renault with his left leg along the back seat. Christie passed out again, fortunately after he had climbed into the front passenger seat. I bumped back across the grass to the road trying not to think of the effect on my passengers' wounds.

When the ME 109s attacked us, we were to the west of Hasselt, and so I calculated that I had about 50 miles to drive to Brussels. I thought I ought to go there for a hospital. It was still brilliantly fine and I set off westwards by keeping the sun on my left in front of me. The road seemed ominously empty, and it was a relief to catch up with two cars travelling together, both with a mattress tied to the roof. Such mattresses were to become a very familiar sight on the refugee cars in the coming weeks. Shortly after I caught up with these cars, I had a most unpleasant fright.

With me behind them, the two cars stopped at a cross-roads, and there we sat for what seemed ages while German tanks and heavy lorries, bristling with soldiers, drove across in front of us. I had feared the Germans might be close, but I had no idea I was already behind their advanced troops. Fortunately these Germans were far too intent on their own affairs to be bothered about three civilian cars, and, when they had passed, we merely drove on past a sign-post which showed we were heading for Louvain and

Brussels. At least I now knew I was going in the right direction, and drove on as quickly as I could without jolting my wounded passengers unduly, overtaking the heavily overloaded refugee cars. My stomach was still churning from the sight of the black crosses on the German vehicles, but I argued philosophically with myself that, as I had to look after my unconscious and wounded crew, I could do little more to escape capture than to stay in the car.

It seemed prudent to drive in my shirt-sleeves. I slipped off the top half of my two-piece flying overalls. With the rank stripe of braid on each shoulder and the pilot's wings, it did seem dangerously conspicuous. With every Germanless mile my confidence increased, and to my great relief, in a village near Louvain, I met British troops, a squadron of cavalry.

At the side of the road was a Whippet tank, a tiny two-man affair, with a subaltern and a corporal standing beside it. I drew up, poked my head out of the window and said, 'You've no idea how pleased I am to see you.' The two soldiers gaped at us.

'Good God! They're British,' cried the subaltern recovering. 'What on earth's happened? Have you seen any Germans?'

By this time I was climbing out of the car and shrugging into the top half of my overalls. 'We were shot down about 30 miles away by some ME 109s,' I said. 'I pinched this car and drove here. I saw a number of German tanks and some motorised infantry about 15 miles back down the road.'

'Well I'm damned,' said the subaltern softly, taking in the blood-soaked state of the motionless Christie and Bence. 'The poor devils.'

'Yes,' I said, 'I've done what I could for them, but they need help.'

'They certainly do,' the subaltern replied, 'and you look in pretty poor shape yourself. But don't let me keep you. Drive on down the street and you'll see our Squadron Headquarters on the left in the village post office. The colonel will have something arranged for you, and he'll be glad to talk to you about what you've seen.'

At the post office I told the colonel my story, pointing out positions as best I could on his map, drinking tea. At intervals a medical orderly was dabbing at my lips and eyes, cleaning them with some disinfectant to remove the viscous fluid which was running out of my blisters. He had also given Christie and Bence morphine injections.

'I wish I could do more for you,' said the colonel, 'but we've only recently arrived. If you can manage to drive on to Louvain, you should see an RAMC casualty clearing station. Good luck!'

I thought of the size of the German tanks and the vehicles carrying their motorised infantry which had passed in front of us at the cross-roads not far away. The colonel's Whippets looked in comparison about as formidable as Austin 7s.

There was a grave expression on his lean, ascetic features and he smiled faintly when I wished him good luck in return. I felt that he and his squadron knew they were doomed, and the thought of them going quietly and gallantly about their tasks still brings a lump into my throat, fifty years later.

Gradually the road became more and more congested with refugees going westwards. My face was beginning to sting and throb. I passed Louvain without any sign of a casualty clearing station, and for want of any other idea, continued on the way to Brussels. A steady stream of people on foot were plodding along the road beside the traffic, lumping suitcases and pushing laden prams. They all seemed to be intent on minding their own business as if survival was a personal affair, not shared with those thronging around them. Houses and shops were shuttered, having every appearance of not wanting to be bothered with the passing flood of unhappy people. Military traffic began to pass in the other direction in increasing quantities, some of which I thought might be my casualty clearing station, and British military policemen were loudly and sweatily in evidence at cross-roads, forcefully keeping traffic moving. It was warm in the afternoon sun.

11 May 1940 – 20.30

A feeling came over me that I was to be a part of this slow, cattle-like movement of people indefinitely; I could not imagine not being part of it. It was now eight-thirty in the evening and I had been up since four-thirty in the morning. I did not feel tired so much as bored, and, I now suppose, it was nervous energy which kept me alert. Suddenly the slow, plodding scene was violently interrupted by a formation of Junkers 87s in the line astern diving on our road, bombing and machine-gunning. Most of the bombs missed the road and the machine-gun bullets swept in a capricious fashion about it. All forward movement stopped, and people dived for cover in a patternless, terrified reaction, knocking into each other. Our car was not touched, but just in front of us a woman carrying a baby was hit in the back, cutting her nearly in two. As she arched back, the baby flew over her shoulder and landed on the paved side-walk. Its head split open. The attack, having come with a shattering tumult of sound, left behind it a momentary motion-less silence. Then, slowly people picked themselves up and started to move on with the cars, stepping over the bodies of the mother and baby.

As we neared the city, the flow of traffic became slower and slower in the subdued lighting which came as night fell. Whereas I had been alert before the JU 87 attack, I now started feeling sleepy, mesmerised by the back of the lorry I was following. With a jerk I pulled myself together, realising that I had forgotten about looking for a hospital and was very vague about how to find one.

Fortunately, I was brought to a halt at a cross-roads by a British military policeman who stepped off the pavement between me and the lorry in front to hold up the traffic. He was one of a group of three. I leaned out of the window and called to the other two on the pavement. 'Would you help me, please?' One came across to me flashing his torch into the Renault as I said, 'I was shot down earlier on and I have to get my crew into a hospital.'

To my amazement he drew himself up and saluted. 'No problem, sir!' The last few hours had been such a shambles that I had forgotten the existence of an orderly world of timetables, meals, daily papers, changes of clothing, and people who were certain. The policeman's salute and the matter-of-fact, easy assurance of his reply was immensely comforting. 'We are just making way for a convoy of Belgian army ambulances and we'll tack you onto the end of them. I'll see to it now. Good luck, sir!' He saluted again and turned away to join his colleague standing in front of me. The policeman on the road looked over his shoulder at me, smiled and nodded. Very shortly afterwards the ambulances arrived, and I was waved forward to follow them. This I did, and after several turns we drew up at a hospital entrance.

11 May 1940 – 22.00

As each ambulance was emptied by an endless chain of stretcher-bearing orderlies in white overalls, those behind moved up one and eventually it was our turn. First Christie was lifted out and put on a stretcher, but as the orderlies were half-way through easing Bence out (he was now semi-conscious and moaning quietly), a uniformed Belgian warrant officer came running down the steps. '*Non! Non!*' he was shouting. '*C'est absolument interdit. Grands blessés militaires seulement.*' My back was turned to him and as I turned round he continued to shout, '*Il faut que vous alliez a un hôpital civilien.*'

The orderlies froze and for a despairing moment, before anger took over, I thought I would have to move miserably on. '*Mon Dieu!*' I shouted back. '*Nous sommes aviateurs anglais! Tombés près de Hasselt! Nous sommes militaires! Je suis officier du* Royal Air Force!' I pointed to the rank stripes on my shoulders and my pilots' wings, and then to Christie and Bence. '*Et certainement ils sont grands blessés.*'

By this time I was standing over Christie's stretcher, and to my delighted amusement I heard his Scots voice saying quietly, 'What's up, sir? Some bloody Frog getting on your wick?' He gave me a faint smile and relapsed into unconsciousness.

The warrant officer was absolutely taken aback. '*Ah!*

pardon, monsieur. Je pense que votre auto...' His voice trailed off as he pointed to the Renault.

He muttered something I could not understand to the orderlies and hurried back up the steps. The now grinning orderlies finished laying Bence out on his stretcher and I followed them up the steps into the hospital.

Inside there, my immediate reaction was one of sympathy for the warrant officer, as I could see only too clearly why he was conscious of the need to limit admittances; there were wounded everywhere. Surgeons and nurses were treating people in surgeries, in consulting rooms, in waiting rooms, in passages and anywhere else a stretcher could be dropped. I looked through a door where something was happening on a table, and, sticking out of an enamel bucket beside it, was an amputated leg. I knew it was a leg because it was still wearing its sock, and boot.

By this time I was beginning to feel light-headed with fatigue. My face was stinging more than ever and the top of my head seemed to be lifting up and down. I sat down on the floor of a corridor beside Christie and Bence and must have dropped off to sleep. I was woken by a nun with an apron over her dark brown habit, shaking my shoulder. Many of the nursing sisters in Belgium were nuns. 'Poor boy! Poor boy!' she was whispering in English. 'Come with me and I shall dress your face.'

'But what about my crew?' I looked at Christie and Bence and saw that they were in garments which looked like night-shirts and that their wounds had been dressed. 'How are they?'

'The one with the head wound has severe concussion. The flesh wound on his forehead has been stitched and all he needs is rest and quiet. But the other' – she paused, looking sadly at Bence – 'the wound in his thigh is very severe, and we can only hope and pray that it will be possible to save his leg. But now, you come with me and you will join them later in a room we have arranged for you three.'

'But I can't stay here,' I cried out. 'I'm all right. If you would just clean up my face, I'll get back to my squadron and tell them what's happened.'

Running through my mind was the old peace-time procedure, 'In the event of a forced landing, make your way to the nearest telephone and report.'

The nun smiled kindly. 'Very well, but come with

me. I think you might as well sleep here when I have finished with you. It is already well past midnight.'

I remember walking along a passage with her holding my arm, having her take my temperature, seeing her shaking her head and hearing her mutter something about '*Quarante*'. I worked out afterwards that my temperature was what we would call 104°.

18 May 1940

The next thing I knew was that I was in a bed in a smallish room which held two other beds containing Christie and Bence. I was in one of the sort of nightshirts which I had seen on the other two. I lay still for some minutes, enjoying feeling cool, clear-headed and rested, but I was very thirsty. I pressed a bell-push which was hanging above me, and shortly afterwards my nun bustled in, took one look at me and cried out in pleasure, 'Ah! I can see you are much better at last!'

'At last?' I was puzzled. 'Why do you say that?'

'My poor boy, you have had a very high temperature and been delirious for seven days.'

'Seven days!' I shot up and immediately sank back again as the nun and the room started spinning. 'Seven days! But I thought I was only here for one night before going back to Poix. What is happening in the war? Where are the Germans?'

'Things are not so good,' she said quietly, 'but you must not worry. You and the other wounded are being taken by a hospital train to a French hospital tonight. Our government is, I believe, moving to Ostend. I shall bring your clothes shortly, but for now what can I do for you?'

'I'm very thirsty.'

'I shall bring you something to drink.' She hurried out, leaving me already beginning to worry about being moved before the Germans overran Brussels, and wondering how I would cope on my own.

The nun came back with some sweet tea and two bundles. By some miracle she had my overalls and Christie's cleaned and pressed, and our shirts and underclothes had been laundered by herself. She was an angel, and I told her so. She smiled and said, 'I wish it was so easy to be an angel.' She told me her name was Sister Adrienne and beamed with pleasure when I told her that my Aunt Alice was an Anglican nun who was also a Sister Adrienne.

The tea looked delicious, but, when I began to drink it, I found the blisters round my mouth had turned into crackly scabs and I had to steer the liquid in as best I could. While I was doing this, Christie opened his eyes looking blankly round.

Sister Adrienne gave him some tea which he drank without a word and lay back. She told me that he was still heavily concussed and did not know what was happening.

Poor Bence was heavily sedated, moaning faintly at intervals.

I was growing more and more anxious about the German advance and about the possibility of being captured. As soon as Sister Adrienne left, I staggered out of bed and had to hang onto the bed-head as my head began to swim. After a while I was able to totter about the room slowly with rests and ventured out into the corridor, but there were so many people scurrying about that I thought it safer, and certainly pleasanter, to return to our room. I dressed slowly into my overalls and flying boots, and it was just as well that I had done so. I had hardly finished when four stretcher bearers, accompanied by Sister Adrienne, arrived for Christie and Bence. She exclaimed with pleasure when she saw me dressed, 'Ah! *Si beau*, I am glad you are dressed. You are now being taken to the station with your two friends. I shall come to see you away.'

I did not feel very *beau*. I now had eight days of stubble growing round and through the scabs on my face, but my overalls at least were clean and someone, probably Sister Adrienne, had cleaned my black leather flying boots, which were shining for the first time ever to my knowledge. With Sister Adrienne beside me, I followed the two stretchers, whose bearers fortunately for me could only make slow progress, down the crowded corridor and stairs, through the entrance hall and down the steps towards the waiting ambulance, one of a line. Christie and Bence were pushed into their places inside, an orderly waving me to follow them, but Sister Adrienne held up her hand.

'*Un moment, s'il vous plaît*,' she said to him, and then leaned to press her cheek against mine. 'My dear boy, *bonne chance, bonne chance*,' she murmured. 'Take these tablets as soon as you are settled in the train, and you will wake up in Amiens.' I gave her a hug and entered the ambulance, exchanging waves with her as the doors were slammed by the orderly who followed me in.

Dear Sister Adrienne! I owed her so much for

taking me under her wing. I found the address of her sisterhood on a card in my pocket. In May 1945, five years later, when I was passing through Brussels on my way home from Germany, I looked for her in her sisterhood. She had died of pneumonia and malnutrition the year before.

In the crowded hospital train, which smelt of disinfectant and suppurating wounds, I found a space in the corridor beside Christie and Bence's stretchers and sat down. I felt awful. With black-out curtains in place, the air was already foul before the journey had started. I was thinking about taking Sister Adrienne's tablets when a fat uniformed Belgian medical officer in shiny field boots and a smart hat with a holstered revolver came bustling importantly along, preceded by an orderly calling out 'Attention! Attention! Le Commandant!'

I thought I ought to stand up, which I did with difficulty in the cramped space, and the commandant stopped when he saw me. 'Ah! Les aviateurs anglais,' he said loudly, his glance taking in the motionless Christie and Bence on their stretchers, and then, changing into English, snapped out staring at me, 'You will understand that on this train you are under my orders and will do as I say.' I was so flabbergasted at being spoken to in this way that I could only give a faint bow. This seemed to satisfy him because, after a steely glare all round, he continued down the corridor. Apart from we three, the other wounded in the coach were all Belgians who were looking at me with interest, some smiling slightly, to see how I was taking this unexpected broadside. I tactfully avoided looking at any of them and sank back to my sitting position, grateful that Christie was not having a momentary period of lucidity; his natural and likely reaction to this pomposity might well have caused Allied discord.

Two orderlies handed out paper cups of lime juice and I took the chance of swallowing Sister Adrienne's tablets. The train moved off shortly afterwards. The only lighting came from a blue bulb at each end of the coach, and in the stinking gloom, with moans and groans all round, feeling uncomfortable, lonely and far from home, I dozed.

Throughout the night I was aware that the train was only travelling slowly and that even this progress was interrupted by clanking halts and starts. At the back of my mind I doubted that we should be anywhere near Amiens, which Sister Adrienne had been told was our destination, three to four hours away. Amiens suited me because it was only 25 miles from Poix and 53 Squadron, which had looked after me for three years. From habit I sought no other haven for Christie, Bence and myself. Amiens, a telephone call, and all would be well.

19 May 1940

In the early dawn of summer I read the name place of the first station we rumbled through after the black-out blinds had been removed. I was shocked and sickened to find we were at Kortrijk and still in Belgium. Although windows were now opened and the atmosphere in the coach had improved, the general conditions in the train had worsened. We had apparently collected refugees, men, women and children, during the night. Many of them were in coaches which had been attached to our train, but some had squashed in with the wounded. Whatever food and drink had been available in Brussels had run out, and the lavatories were all hopelessly blocked. There was no sign of any medical attention in our coach and I thought bitterly about our fat commandant and his revolver. What had he been doing?

Throughout that hot summer day, I busied myself doing what I could for Christie and Bence. There were bed-bottles in our coach and, when occasionally my two used them, I dumped the contents out of the windows. I found an empty flask and whenever the train stopped at a station, at a level crossing or at a signal box, I refilled it. That flask was invaluable because at the stops no one was parting with any utensils, and it was the only means I had of conveying liquids to my patients. Christie did not trouble me too much because only intermittently did he know what was happening, but poor young Bence was in agony when he was conscious.

It was not possible to move through the packed train. As soon as I realised that any help for him depended on me, when the train made one of its frequent stops I jumped down onto the side of the track and hurried along the train calling for a doctor. When I found one I pleaded with him to give Bence some morphia or other injection to knock him out. The doctor was frantically busy, but he did send a not very willing orderly with me to give Bence a heavy dose of morphia. By now I was pleased to be feeling stronger.

At level crossings we would pass lines of refugee

cars with the now familiar mattresses on their roofs waiting to continue their south-westerly journeys. Many of these cars had small Belgian pennants fluttering on their bonnets. Drivers and their passengers would stand waving and cheering at our train, and those who could waved and called back. What any of them were waving and cheering about, I could not think. I felt that many of them were near hysteria.

As all the lavatories were blocked, when the train stopped people would clamber out to relieve themselves on either side of the track. The convention of males to the right and females to the left was quickly adopted. I had read about this being the custom on the wagon-trains and stage-coaches of the old Wild West. In this instance the wide spaces below the coach floors and between the wheels provided little modesty cover for the squatting travellers.

When we crossed into France, which we did at about midday, there was no more waving. Shops or cafes near the railway were almost always shut. People went about their own affairs sullenly, paying little or no attention to us. There was little military activity of any sort, and no policemen were to be seen. Whenever we stopped in a town I looked in vain for a baker, a milkman, or a newsagent. I was puzzled by the abnormal atmosphere. Up to 10 May people lived their usual lives as far as wartime conditions allowed, but now no longer. We seemed to be lumbering slowly through a shadowy, unrealistic world, full of pain.

We reached St Omer in the evening and it was strange for me to realise that only two weeks before I had played rugby there for a Royal Air Force team against l'Armée du Nord, before a vocally partisan crowd of 10,000. When the train stopped in the station, the word went round that we would be there for some time. My first task was to fill the flask, which I did at a tap in the waiting room, and then, when still no movement of the train seemed likely, I thought I would try and find out what was happening. After I went to the station-master's office to find it was locked, I went to the locomotive thinking that the driver might have an idea of when we might move and if we were still heading for Amiens. The cab was empty.

At this stage I was tempted to push off and find my own way, but the thought of the defenceless Christie and Bence brought me up short, and I walked along the train hoping to see the commandant. I learned that several of his staff had arranged dinner at a hotel in the town. How could he ignore the grim condition of many of the wounded in his charge, Bence in particular? I hoped his meal would choke him.

As I was walking back gloomily towards our coach, I was stopped by what I thought was a typical French peasant lady in a black shapeless dress and shawl with a large cardboard box under one arm.

'So they were right!' she cried in English. 'I heard that there were some RAF wounded on the train, and came down hoping you might like some of these.'

She pulled a cloth off the top of the box to reveal a large number of eggs, and seeing I was taken aback, added, smiling:

I'm English though I know I don't look it. I'm married to a farmer near here. The market has not been held and the shops who take our eggs haven't opened. They will be going to waste. Please take them. Even if you can't cook them, they'll do you good raw.

'How very kind of you!' I said, overcoming my surprise at this strange encounter. 'I only wish I could pay you for them, but I have no money. Nor have we anything to eat.' We had had some thick soup before leaving the hospital, but nothing since, and I suddenly realised that I was indeed very hungry. We parted, exchanging good wishes, and I carried the box in triumph to our coach, inviting the occupants to share them. I used a pencil to tap a hole in the end of an egg and sucked out the contents. They were delicious, and I dealt with two more eggs in a like manner.

To my relief Christie was awake and clear-headed, for the time being at any rate. I fed him three eggs and explained to him that I was trying to find out what was happening. He was astounded to learn that we had been shot down in the week before; the last thing he could remember was giving me a small alteration of heading on our final photographic run. Until I came back to the coach, he had been trying to puzzle out what he was doing on a stretcher with his head in bandages wearing a night-shirt. I suggested that he might try to stand up, and perhaps take a step or two in preparation for leaving the train if that was what we ought to do.

To my surprise, when I was back on the platform, I saw a light on in the station-master's office and hurried over to it. Crazy and unreal as my life seemed to have become, the scene in the office was bedlam. Seated behind the desk in uniform with a smart hat was obviously the station-master, but he was paying no attention to the four other occupants, who were in overalls and soft caps with shiny peaks, obviously foot-plate men. I shortly found out that they were the Belgian driver and fireman of our locomotive who were waiting to go back to Brussels, and the French driver and fireman who were taking over from them. All four were sniggering and grinning at the station-master who was alternately throwing his arms in the air and thumping his desk. He was shouting over and over again '*Moi, je suis cocu. Moi, je suis cocu.*'

As there was no prospect of finding out anything from him, I followed the four foot-plate men out of the office. When they had stopped giggling enough to talk to me, I learned that the poor station-master, having been on duty continuously for more than twenty-four hours, had gone home for a meal and a rest only to find his wife in bed with a neighbour. It was laboriously and carefully explained to me that *cocu* meant cuckolded.

The two pairs of foot-plate men wished each other good luck and parted, and I followed the French pair towards the locomotive. Hoping at least he would know, I asked the engine driver where the train was going. To my relief he said that he lived in Amiens and so he was going there. In the chaotic circumstances, at first this seemed to me to be a reasonable and practical answer, particularly as I had understood from Sister Adrienne that the wounded on the train were expected at the hospital there. It was only later that I realised how fortunate it was for me and my crew that the driver did not live in Calais or Arras.

While I was talking to the driver, I noticed the wretched commandant and his staff returning and climbing into their coach at the end of the train. After about half an hour we clanked away into the night for another slow journey punctuated by unexplained delays. Christie and I had some more eggs; I did what little I could for Bence, who was fortunately unconscious; and I settled down to doze as best I could.

20 May 1940

By mid-morning we were near the sea south of Boulogne. I had an idea that the British Expeditionary Force had hospitals positioned along this coastline and I began to think about abandoning the Belgian medical arrangements and the possibility of having Christie and Bence transferred to a British hospital before we reached Amiens. Christie had become vague again, but I did persuade him that if he were dressed it would be easier to deal with one stretcher instead of two. Sister Adrienne had attached his overalls and underclothes in a parcel to his stretcher, and, after a struggle on the part of both of us, he was lying on his stretcher fully dressed.

The chance I was hoping for came when our train pulled into a station and stopped. I saw the name Étaples with some interest as I had often read about the notorious British Expeditionary Force training base there in the First World War, called the Bull-Ring by the unhappy soldiers who had suffered in it. A Belgian orderly came running down the platform crying '*Cinq minutes! Cinq minutes!*' which I took to mean we were having a short stop in the station.

In the station courtyard I saw with a wave of relief two British army ambulances and hurried over to them through the crowd of passengers who were swarming over the platform. I was feeling so much better by now that I kept forgetting about the effect my desperate appearance had on people who were suddenly confronted by me. The look on the faces of the ambulance party reminded me. The Royal Army Medical Corps corporal in charge eyed me with puzzled concern as he saluted me. 'Whatever has happened to you, sir? Aren't there any medical facilities on that train?'

'Precious little,' I replied, 'but I'm all right although I must look pretty grim. It's my navigator and air-gunner who badly need attention. Can you help?'

'We're from No. 1 Base Hospital at Berck Plage. We've been waiting here since early morning for a train of our wounded from Belgium, but it's long overdue. No one seems to know what's going on.'

'Would one of your ambulances take my two to your hospital?' I asked.

'Yes,' he replied. 'We'll come right away.'

I hurried back to our coach to prepare Christie and Bence for their removal. Christie still had a vague look when I started speaking, but his brain seemed to clear as he said, 'I think I'll manage fine without a stretcher.' He and I stepped out of the coach, and I waved to my ambulance corporal, who was leading four orderlies with two stretchers through the station entrance onto the platform.

At this moment I heard angry shouting coming from the rear end of the train and saw to my horror the fat commandant with three of his staff running down the platform shaking his fist at me and loudly demanding to know what was happening.

I explained that there was an ambulance ready to take Christie and Bence to Berck Plage and that I was going with them before making my way to 53 Squadron at Poix. '*Absolument interdit,*' he screamed. He drew his revolver and waved it at me. '*Entrez le train immédiatement.*' He was so excited that anything could have happened.

I turned to the RAMC corporal who was behind me and muttered, 'We'll have to leave it. We'll never be able to get my men out of the train without someone being shot.'

'OK, sir,' said the corporal quietly out of the corner of his mouth, looking at no one in particular and shrugging. 'The fat idiot must be pissed. Good luck! We'll be waiting by the ambulances.' He and his party pushed their way through the dense and intensely interested crowd which had gathered. The commandant, revolver still dangerously at the ready, waved me onto the train. I looked round for Christie, but, as the commandant was advancing on me, I decided discretion to be the thing for the time being and jumped into the open doorway of my coach. As I did so, out of the corner of my eye I saw Christie melting into the background behind the onlookers. The heavily scowling commandant seemed to be about to say something to me, but mercifully the engine driver blew a sharp blast on his whistle and the train gave one or two preliminary jolts. The commandant and his posse turned tail and hurried down the platform to their carriage at the rear. As they climbed into it, the train started. As soon as I was sure it was on its way I jumped back onto the platform and darted across it into the shelter of the station buildings, followed by cheers and laughter from the onlookers.

I hated leaving Bence but I was worried about Christie, who was in no state to look after himself, and I thought that, as the train driver was heading for Amiens and home, I could have Bence rescued there by a 53 Squadron ambulance as originally I had planned. I looked around for Christie but there was no sign of him, and in fact I never saw him again. Sometime later I heard that he had been found wandering around near Boulogne in a dazed state and evacuated to England on one of the last ships to leave before the Germans arrived there on 24 May. He was killed over Berlin later on in the war. I liked him very much indeed. In all the long, sometimes testing hours we had spent together, he remained courteous, helpful and unruffled. There are not many like him.

In the station yard I saw a door with RTO on it in large letters, and thankfully headed for it. Whenever considerable numbers of British troops used a railway station, a railway transport officer was installed to supervise travel arrangements, and here I found a Sapper lieutenant. 'Good God!' he greeted me, jumping to his feet. 'What on earth's happened to you?' I had again forgotten about my unshaven, scabby face and my overalls, dusty and crumpled after two days of sitting in the corridor of the train.

'I was shot down near Hasselt on 11 May, and I'm heading for Poix to rejoin 53 Squadron. May I put a call through to them?'

The RTO gaped at me, speechless at first, and then said, 'Where have you been? Haven't you heard what's been happening?'

'For the last nine days I've been in hospital in

Brussels and in that hospital train commanded by a fat lunatic. Tell me, is the news bad?'

He looked grim.

It could scarcely be worse. The Germans are swarming through the Ardennes into east Belgium and north France. The BEF's falling back towards the coast. Your squadron's ground crew, and those of the other RAF units in this area, have been going through here on their way to Boulogne for the last night and day. I believe the aircraft have already gone. We're pulling out tomorrow.

That was how I learned of the extent of the catastrophe which had befallen the Allies. I asked the lieutenant where the nearest RAF squadron was. He shrugged his shoulders but gave me a mug of tea and a bully-beef sandwich. Then, having made a telephone call, he turned back to me. '13 Squadron is still operating at Crécy and isn't leaving until first thing tomorrow.'

Crécy, I thought. We might have won a famous battle there in 1346, but that was not going to be repeated in 1940. I thanked the Sapper lieutenant for his help and hospitality and left wishing him good luck. Although most of the military vehicles on the main road outside the station were going north in the direction of Boulogne, the Royal Military Police directing traffic said there were occasional staff cars or ambulances going south towards Crécy, and promised to stop something for me.

Greatly depressed and worried, I hung around near them. I had lost Christie and poor, young, stoical Bence was going towards Amiens where no 53 Squadron would be on hand to rescue him. I could only hope that some medical attention would be given to him, even if by Germans, before it was too late. I learned months later that his leg had been amputated only a little below his thigh, and that he had been taken prisoner in hospital.

<hr>

I next saw Bence in 1982 in North Yorkshire where I was living, and where he was visiting relatives. By accident he had learned my address, and had come belatedly, to thank me for saving his life. He was now living in Gloucestershire, a retired schoolmaster. I was delighted to see him if only to be able to tell him that for forty-two years I had been wishing I could have done more to help him, and would continue to do so. It was a tonic to see him so cheerful and so little changed in spirit from my eighteen-year-old air-gunner in spite of all that had happened to him.

How lucky I had been to have had Christie and him as my crew for the two years we were together.

The lack of local life in France, which had been puzzling me on the journey from the Belgian frontier, was evident in Étaples. I now realised the reason lay in the war news which the RTO had given me. The local people, never enthusiastic about the war, had given up. Very few people were about, and those that were took no notice of us. They looked apathetic, not so much downcast by disaster as indifferent to events. A school closed for the day, and the children, instead of erupting noisily, hurried silently home. Few shops were open, and I saw no sign of policemen. Until what they obviously considered to be the inevitable arrival of the German army, people, it seemed, were conserving their resources, waiting to see what would happen.

Eventually the military police stopped an RAF ambulance heading south, and I climbed into it. It was in fact from 13 Squadron and had been taking wounded aircrew to hospital. On the way back to Crécy the ambulance broke down, and, after the driver had cleaned out the carburettor, we limped towards the airfield, which we reached just after darkness fell.

I was dropped at the officers' mess in an old farmhouse on the edge of the airfield. There was every sign of an imminent removal. At the bar, which had been built in one of the rooms, I saw to my pleasure four or five familiar faces from the members of 13 Squadron, which with 4 Squadron had shared Odiham with us.

On my appearance there was a moment of silence before I was greeted variously.

'Alastair! You look like Frankenstein!'

'We were told you had had it.'

'It's good to see you.'

'What happened, for God's sake?'

I became the centre of a chattering throng which was joined by strangers to me who were inquisitive about the scruffy, scabby, unshaven flying officer who had suddenly appeared out of the darkness. I learned very quickly how very sad the news was. 53 Squadron had indeed flown back to England, to Tangmere, they thought, that morning, less about half the friends I had left ten days before.

13 Squadron had been equally hard hit, and were, as the RTO at Étaples had thought, leaving early in the morning. A buffet of soup and bully-beef shepherd's pie, delicious it tasted to me, was announced, and we continued our exchange of news between mouthfuls.

There was a motley collection of pilots in the mess, refugees from various situations, and one of these, a quiet, slim flight lieutenant, stranded from a Hurricane fighter squadron, took me aside when he heard I was a Blenheim pilot.

He explained that that morning six Blenheims had been delivered at Crécy from an aircraft storage unit in England before the arrangements could be altered. If no one could be found to fly them to England the next day, they would have to be burned. He asked if I would show him around the cockpit and tell him as much as I could what to do. Did I think he had a reasonable chance of taking one of the Blenheims safely back to England? At least then he and I would save two of the six. Full of beer, soup and shepherd's pie, relaxed by being back among my own kind, and relieved by now knowing how I would be able to make my own way home, I assured him laughingly that he should have no trouble. I had little justification for being so confident, but in the general mayhem, all sorts of normally unacceptable risks were being taken.

After a cup of coffee, he and I went across to the aircraft parked round the airfield, and climbed into the first Blenheim, having borrowed a torch from some ground crew. We found the manual, Blenheim Pilot's Notes, and I went through the starting, take-off and landing procedures with him, showing him the positions and operation of the various levers and switches. The main problem was that he had only flown single-engined aircraft before, and the Blenheim was a twin. We discussed how he should manage the two engines, and after an hour I left him. I wanted some sleep and he wanted to sit in the cockpit going over the Pilot's Notes.

I arranged to meet him at four o'clock when we thought it would be light enough to see the obstructions round the airfield. Crécy might have been a good site 600 years earlier for a pitched battle between armoured knights and archers, but, from what we had learned, it was none too big for a Blenheim to take off safely. In the mess I found an empty sofa and was soon asleep.

21 May 1940

Well before dawn I was woken by the noise of bustling people preparing to depart, and was told that the commanding officer of 13 Squadron had asked to see me when I awoke. I found him looking very sad, and very, very tired, but he smiled warmly at me and said how glad he was I was still alive. He had found another stray from a Hurricane squadron who had volunteered to join my Hurricane pilot in taking a Blenheim back to England if I would 'show him round the office' as he put it. I, of course, readily agreed. The squadron leader with a wry smile then said, 'You know about burning Blenheims, I understand. Would you set fire to the three remaining ones before you take off?'

I had been thinking about this sad waste of new aircraft and asked him if he could say how long he thought it would be before the Germans arrived.

'Official intelligence information', he said, 'is non-existent. My estimate is based on what we have been seeing for ourselves from the air. Of course, I can't be sure, but I think it will be two or three days before advance units of the German army arrive at the coast. We're in a hurry to return the squadron to England, not immediately because of being over-run by the Germans, but to start operating from there in support of the BEF under some co-ordinated plan. It's maddening. We've had no requests for sorties from here for two days now, and I'm sure there's more than enough needed to be done.'

'Well, sir,' I said, 'it looks as if we have at least today in hand. If I take off at five, I'll be at Tangmere by six and there will be plenty of time to pick up three other Blenheim pilots and return here for the three remaining Blenheims later today.'

He looked at me for a moment, smiling. 'Very well. I would not have asked you to do that, but I'll leave it to you. Now, off you go. We have both a good deal to do. Good luck.'

'Thank you, sir.' I turned away, but he stopped me, putting a hand on my shoulder. 'Don't forget I'm only guessing about the German advance. Have a good look round the area before you land back here.' In the event the squadron leader's estimate was a very good one. Three days later, on 24 May, the Germans entered Boulogne.

I found my two Hurricane pilots in the first Blenheim where they had been quizzing each other from the Pilot's Notes. As a result I did not have to spend much time talking to the second volunteer. We commandeered a truck, and drove round the airfield as dawn was breaking and chose the longest available run. It was adequate, but no more. I then supervised the starting of the other two Blenheims' engines and watched them taxi slowly and gingerly. They waited for me at our chosen take-off point and followed me into the air.

I had a great deal of trouble pulling my Blenheim off the ground, and only just cleared the trees beyond the edge of the airfield at the far end. Because of this I was very relieved to see, on circling round, that the other two were airborne without apparent trouble. We had arranged to make for Shoreham, which was the recognised English end of the ferry route to France. The other two followed me as they thought they would like to leave finding the way to me so that they could concentrate on flying their aircraft.

As usual with new aircraft from storage units, our

Blenheims had no radio means of identification. To avoid being attacked by our own fighters we arranged to fly at 1,000 feet with lowered undercarriages when we neared the Sussex coast. All went according to plan. We crossed at Shoreham on a lovely still morning, leaving Beachy Head on our right.

England looked unbelievably calm and peaceful as we turned west along the coast to Tangmere, near Chichester. With some admiration I circled to watch my two 'pupils' land bumpily but safely. After my take-off, I had continued to be aware of how heavy and sluggish my Blenheim felt; whenever I throttled back a little I lost height immediately. I had three airmen in the cockpit with me; they had asked if I would give them a lift back to avoid travelling via Boulogne. Over Tangmere, by force of habit, I turned to read the cylinder-head temperature gauges over my right shoulder; their reading was needed in the post-flight report; but I was amazed to see three faces in a row behind me, peering ahead and grinning.

'If there are any others behind them,' I thought, 'it's no wonder the aircraft feels sluggish; I must be heavily overloaded.' I approached and landed at much higher speed than usual to avoid sinking. When I parked, I switched off and left the cockpit, followed by my three cockpit companions. I waited by the air-gunner's hatch for my three stowaways, only to be staggered when nine airmen in all climbed stiffly out. They must have slipped in after I had started up. How on earth they had all found room for their bodies, I could not think. My stowaways were stretching and rubbing themselves, laughing with relief and delight at being back in England so quickly and safely, and clustered round to thank me for the lift. Truly, in their case, ignorance was bliss. If one engine had failed …

'Why didn't you divide yourselves up among the three Blenheims,' I asked, 'instead of all piling into mine? I was dangerously overloaded.'

A corporal grinned at me cheerfully. 'You wouldn't think to catch us cadging trips off sprogs, would you, sir? We knew we would be OK with you!'

The quiet orderliness of Tangmere in the early morning sunshine made it difficult to believe what chaos existed across the Channel. The off-going night watch, while looking forward to being relieved and having breakfast, were going methodically about their tasks. In the Station Operations Room the duty officer took charge of me. He telephoned the storage unit to ensure that there would be no more deliveries of Blenheims to Crécy; he rang up Andover for three Blenheim pilots to come to Tangmere as quickly as possible; he arranged for my Blenheim to be serviced; and he ordered an early breakfast for me in the mess. Then he turned to me. 'The mess steward wants to know how you would like your eggs done.'

'Scrambled, please,' I said, laughing inwardly. The duty officer was a very pukka sahib, and if I told him that the last eggs I had eaten I had sucked out of a hole in the shell made by my pencil, he would surely question my officer qualities.

I landed back at Crécy at about ten o'clock, with the three pilots for the three remaining Blenheims, shortly before the last of 13 Squadron pulled out on their way to Hawkinge, near Folkestone. While the three Blenheims were being serviced, I slipped into Crécy village with the squadron adjutant, who had some job to do there. Tired-looking refugees were still going southwards on the main road. Shops were closed and many houses were shuttered. The few villagers to be seen had, I thought, an oddly furtive appearance. When I remarked on this to the adjutant, he told me that they were probably hiding bread and milk under their coats or cloaks. Any bread or milk available was issued to locals only through back doors, and care was being taken to share nothing with refugees. I noticed the reaction to us was the same as in Étaples the day before, only more pronounced. People were going to some lengths to avoid having anything to do with us; we were no longer good news.

My return to Tangmere with four 13 Squadron ground crew was uneventful. I was kept busy being questioned by intelligence officers, and having my face tidied up by the station medical officer, before being given five days' sick leave.

My immediate reaction was to telephone my Aunt Bessie in Aberdeenshire to ask her for a bed. When I was four years old in Bengal, my mother and my father, who was Aunt Bessie's brother, died in a cholera epidemic. Aunt Bessie became my guardian and the guardian of my brother Colin, five years my senior, and now a captain in the Gordon Highlanders. She was now married to a doctor, Donald Malcolm. I heard her telephone ringing and then her voice. 'Mrs Malcolm here'.

'It's Alastair. I…'

'Alastair! Alastair! My dear boy! My dearest boy! Is

it really you? Are you really all right? We thought you had been killed!'

'Yes, I'm fine! I really am, but...'

'I had a casualty next-of-kin telegram saying you were missing believed killed on 11 May. That was ten days ago. Where have you been? What's been happening?

'Oh, how marvellous! I'm so happy! When can we see you?'

'I've been given five days' sick leave. I can catch the overnight King's Cross train and should be with you tomorrow morning. May I stay with you? Is that all right?'

'Of course it is! I should have hated it if you didn't come to us! Oh! Glory be!'

'Darling aunt! See you soon!'

I realised then that 53 Squadron, wherever it was, did not yet know I was back in England. As far as I was concerned that could be sorted out later. Others could do the battling for Britain for a bit. I had five days' sick leave and was off home.

In the later afternoon train to Waterloo it did not seem real to be sitting in a first-class carriage which rolled smoothly along; to have people smiling kindly at me in my battered and bandaged state; to cross

London by taxi and have the driver refuse to take money; to have strangers wanting to buy me a drink; to have the overnight Edinburgh train leaving King's Cross on time; to have Aunt Bessie and Donald Malcolm making a fuss of me on the platform at Aberdeen station the next morning; and to be driven through the sunny, silent countryside to Craigwell, their house near Kintore, with its garden sloping gently down to the river Don.

On the way, as soon as there was a pause in Aunt Bessie's breathless interrogation, I was able to ask, 'What news of Colin?'

Donald answered. 'You know that his battalion was detached to the Maginot Line for a spell of duty there? Well, we've heard that was cut short and that they are back in north France somewhere with the BEF again. We've heard nothing since.'

'It's all very vague and worrying. I hate not knowing about my two boys.' Then Aunt Bessie's sad voice and her concerned expression brightened. 'But at least I've got you where I can see you and spoil you for a few short days!'

Page from the RAF Operations Record Book detailing Alastair Panton's flight on 11 May 1940 – note in the remarks section: 'Aircraft Failed to Return.'

This is the Blenheim Alastair flew on 11 May 1940, after it fell.

Photograph kindly supplied and reproduced with permission of Peter Cornwell,
author of *The Battle of France, Then and Now*.

CHAPTER 3

DUNKIRK INTERLUDE

At the end of my five days' sick leave, I rejoined 53 Squadron, now also at Hawkinge with 13 Squadron, having called in at the Air Ministry in Kingsway on my way through London to find out where the squadron was. The first officer I saw was Jasper Johns, one of the few friends surviving from 11 May. He was wearing a smart pair of Poulsen and Skone brogues which belonged to me. Just before he left Poix he had found them in our flight's Nissen hut where I had changed them for my flying boots on 11 May. We had a hilarious restoration of my property.

'I never thought you would need them again.' Jasper was grinning and laughing. 'And you'd better have your sunglasses too,' he added, pulling them from a pocket. The shoes and sunglasses were the only items of my kit from Poix which were saved. When the order to pull out of Poix and return to England was given, there was just time for most of the squadron technical equipment to be packed onto the motor transport before it set off for Boulogne. Our ground crews had performed prodigies of labour to save as much as possible, all to no purpose.

A sergeant fitter, who had been in my flight the whole time since I joined it, and whom I admired for his knowledge, skill and immense capacity for hard work, later told me what had happened.

We were told it was vital to save as much as possible; I drove a tractor, towing a petrol-bowser, all the way from Poix to Boulogne with six airmen sitting on the catwalk on each side of the bowser with their tool boxes. I tell you, sir, it was diabolical. Bloody uncomfortable all the time, hot in the day, bitterly cold at night, no food, refugees everywhere, and hard even to get water to drink. Then, when we got to Boulogne harbour, and I had just said to the erks 'Well, lads, we've done it. We got the perishing things here. Gerry won't get them', some sodding embarkation officer tells us to drive the lot into the harbour. 'No room on board for anything except personnel and personal weapons.' Cor! I could have kicked him in his personal weapon.

I imagine that my kit, carefully packed in my tin trunk by my batman, helped by a grieving Madame Foullens, had probably joined the bowser and tractor in Boulogne harbour, if it had not been burned at Poix as non-essential stores.

Among the aircrew in the squadron were many new faces replacing the casualties we had suffered, and I was flattered to find how I was looked up to by the newcomers as an experienced veteran whose advice was worth having. Some years later, I met one of these replacement pilots. 'You'll be amused to know,' he said laughing, 'we all thought what a gen man you were. For years afterwards, whenever I was faced with a problem in the air, I found myself thinking "What would Panton do now?"'

After various reconnaissance flights over north France during the past five days, the squadron was now back to full strength and capability for the next day. On the BBC nine o'clock news, we heard that there had been a service of intercession and prayer in Westminster Abbey that afternoon for the BEF. Wondering what was in store for us, we hoped the prayers might cover us too. That evening the squadron commander called all aircrew into the Operations

Room to tell us that the BEF were now almost surrounded, the French First Army having broken on their right, and were fighting their way to the coast in the Dunkirk area in the hope that some of them could be evacuated from there.

Things looked grim indeed.

At this briefing I met my new navigator and air-gunner, both straight from training. Sergeant Farrow from Dumfries was twenty-five, and the 24-year-old Sergeant Stride was a Canadian who had enlisted in the Royal Air Force.

We flew two sorties on 27 May, one in the morning and one in the later afternoon, over the west flank of the BEF. In the morning we flew round and round our area of St Omer, Aire and Merville, reporting the position of all troops, German and British, which we saw. We were low down, at about 800 feet most of the time, being fired at indiscriminately, but fortunately not effectively, by both sides who were more occupied firing at each other. There seemed to be a good deal of air activity high above us which we ignored in our preoccupation with pinpointing troops by map reading. In the afternoon we covered the area of Armentières, Menin and Ypres, all famous First

World War names. During both sorties we had cameras working most of the time, and we hoped that these, together with the many map references of troop positions we gave to the intelligence officers awaiting our return, would still be of value to our customers, whoever they were, by the time they received them. We were not optimistic; the situation seemed to be changing very quickly.

I had told Stride to forget about his radio and concentrate on watching our tail. He saw nothing to fire at and felt left out of things. He was full of fight, and cheered up when the ground crew pointed out little clusters of bullet holes in the skin of the Blenheim near his turret.

After dinner, five or six of us walked down to the village pub through the still evening for beer and darts. It took a while for our minds to absorb the pleasant and peaceful scene in the pub; the mass of German armour we had been seeing all day made us very anxious. When a well-dressed man came into the pub to buy cigarettes, he saw us and frowned. 'I'm surprised you can spare the time to be here,' he said. 'I should have thought you would be helping our soldiers.'

Jasper spun round on him. 'We've been at it all day,' he snapped. 'There's very little we could do now and we'll be at it again tomorrow.'

One of the others added, 'We'll be back tomorrow evening with a bit of luck.'

The well-dressed man flushed. 'I'm sorry. I should have thought, but I've two sons in the Gunners and I can only hope. It's agony waiting.' I followed him outside and wished him and his sons good luck, and told him I found it strange and unreal to be enjoying visits to the pub between visits to the grimness of the battlefield. He pressed my arm, and walked quickly away.

In another sortie on 28 May over the area covering the east flank of the BEF, which was becoming easier for us to work in as it became familiar, we were greatly encouraged to see that the BEF was indeed moving in a body towards the sea. When we returned, however, we learned that the Belgian army had capitulated on the personal authority of their King, leaving the north-west flank of the BEF exposed. All day the escape of the BEF seemed to be in the balance.

For our next sortie we were switched to new ground on the north-west flank to the Ostend, Nieuwpoort, Diksmuide area, but we were unable to detect any German activity of note. This evidently surprised our interrogators, and we were sent back as quickly as we could turn round for the third sortie. Again we were not able to detect much German activity and the photographs we had taken earlier supported us. We did, however, report that considerable British forces had arrived between Nieuwpoort, Furnes and Bergues. Our report confirmed other reports coming in, some from the BEF itself, and was the subject of much satisfaction. For the first time we heard about the formation of the Dunkirk perimeter to allow evacuation to take place from the beaches contained by it, as well as from the port of Dunkirk itself. The evacuation, which had started on the night 26–7 May, was now gathering momentum as all manner of ships and boats collected in Channel ports for despatch to the beaches.

We went to our village pub again that night, but it was more a gesture of bravado than anything else; we were very tired. We were, however, quicker than the night before to settle down to enjoy the peace of the pub and the fine evening. Also, there were more locals there and the growing optimism about the BEF was evident in the tone of the conversations. It was pleasant to grin back at people who wished us luck and told us to keep it up, and to know that some people realised we were hard at work, even if they learned it from us. We all slept well after the relaxation.

When we reported to the Operations Room for early briefing on 29 May, the change of atmosphere was immediately apparent, as it had been in the pub the evening before. All uncertainty about positions and tasks was over. There was no longer any talk about the feasibility of a large evacuation. The operation was an established fact, and the issue for us had simplified. The more German bombers our fighters could knock down, and the more the German army could be attacked, the more of the BEF could be evacuated. Reconnaissance and photography was no longer required of us and it was now a case of Madame Foullens' *'Crackez les Boches.'*

In the small hours of the morning, our ground

crews had been busy bombing up our aircraft, and our instructions were uncomplicated. The German field batteries were making life on the beaches uncomfortable; we were given a target area just east of Nieuwpoort and told to bomb any German gun positions we could see. It was a heady, exciting role. All that hot day the attacks continued by a variety of aircraft from England. All our attacks were low-level ones carried out at 200 feet, a method which gave us maximum flexibility; we picked a target and flew straight at it and over it low down, releasing bombs to arrive on the target more or less at the same time as we passed over it. Low-level bombing was the only method I had practised. As for Farrow and Stride, they had never seen bombs before, let alone been in an aircraft dropping them, and they became increasingly enthusiastic as the day wore on. We made three sorties, all in the Nieuwpoort area, hammering away at German gun positions. On the way to and from our target areas, we could see the lines of shipping crossing and recrossing the Channel; bombs and shells exploding among the lines of soldiers on the beaches, and around the shipping standing off them; and air battles in the blue sky above us. It was a gigantic, awesome panorama.

On our third sortie, an extraordinary thing happened. Having lined up my target, I found I was following another Blenheim from an unknown squadron. Not knowing what delay had been set on his bombs, and not wanting to be blown up by them, I eased off to his port side. As I pressed my release button, the other Blenheim's bombs exploded, and as I passed over the German guns, a soldier appeared in the air beside our cockpit 200 feet up, still running, with a ludicrous look of outraged surprise on his face which I could clearly see under his helmet.

We were much more lively in the pub that night, but sad about Jasper Johns, who had not returned from his first sortie. Just before closing time, however, Jasper appeared looking very salt-stained and bedraggled, shouting for a pint.

One of his engines had been hit by ack-ack fire, and, losing height steadily, he made his way back across the Channel, aiming to ditch as close to the coast as possible. Just as he was preparing to do this, the Goodwin Sands appeared before him in the ebbing tide and he flopped onto them, where later he was joined by a German Heinkel. The two crews glowered at each other 200 yards apart until a fishing boat from

Margate appeared. Jasper and his two sergeants waded out to the boat, which was full of battered-looking soldiers from the beaches, but the Germans refused to be rescued, presumably hoping to be rescued from drowning by a German boat.

Jasper said that he had had a very cool reception from the soldiers, who, on landing at Margate, had given three cheers for the navy, three more for the fishermen, and three boos for us.

Jasper's treatment by the soldiers was our first direct experience of the bitterness towards us on the part of the returning BEF, who were infuriated by the praise we were getting from the BBC, which they put down to propaganda. It was understandable that the soldiers should feel as they did; the only aircraft they saw were German ones because we were operating out of sight, above and beyond them. Nevertheless, it was galling for us in view of the casualties we were suffering, very galling, and the record needed to be put straight.

Full of enthusiasm for another day's bombing, on 30 May we set off early for our first sortie. The day before, east of Nieuwpoort, Farrow had pinpointed a German battery which had incurred his particular animosity by the enthusiasm which it seemed to have for firing. He checked that it was still there on our arrival in the area, and I carried out my usual curving approach towards it. Mercifully, I was flying westwards when I flattened out for my run in, because, just as I released our stick of bombs, there was a loud crash underneath my seat, something flashed upwards between my thighs and disappeared out of the cockpit hatch above my head. At the same time the control column and rudder bar flapped loosely. Instinctively I opened the throttles to full power, and we climbed away.

Farrow had been lying flat on the cockpit floor, looking back through the hatch cover. I heard him in my headphone shout, 'Super! We got the bastards bang on!'

'Never mind about that,' I replied. 'We are in the shit ourselves.'

'What's happened?' I heard Farrow's voice, suddenly anxious, no longer triumphant, as he looked up and round at me.

'Come and see,' I replied. He came and stood beside me, reconnecting his intercom lead, and I pointed to the hole in the floor between my legs behind the control column, and in the hatch above my head. 'It must have been an ack-ack shell which didn't explode. I have no aileron, elevator or rudder control. The shell has severed the lot. But I can keep straight and climb with the engines and, thank God, we are pointing for home.'

'That's not the only thing to thank him for.' Farrow was laughing. 'Look at your thigh straps. Another inch and you'd have lost your tackle.' I looked down and gasped and shivered. The two straps of my parachute harness inside the tops of my thighs had a brown mark where the shell had passed between them.

Oh so near! We soon crossed the coast leaving Dunkirk and the shipping plying across the Channel on our left, climbing steadily.

'What happens now, sir?' Stride, marooned in his turret behind us, had been listening to us.

'Well,' I replied, 'I've been thinking about that. One thing's certain. I'm not going to try to land on the engines alone. We'll have to bale out. We should be at about 8,000 feet by the time we reach Kent, but I'm not sure where we're heading.' As I was talking Farrow had been returning to his navigation table in the nose and, when I saw he had plugged in his intercom lead, I asked him to plot our track on our existing heading. Very soon he had drawn a line on his map which he held up for me to see. 'I thought as much,' I went on. 'We're heading for south London as we are now. By throttling down on the port engine we should be able to turn to port enough for the aircraft to fly out to sea somewhere over the Sussex coast.' This is what we did. Very gingerly, I carried out a turn to port through about 40 degrees. Indeed, I was not at all sure that I could bring the aircraft straight and level without any controls when I reopened the port engine, but in the event we came out of the turn very smoothly.

Somewhere between Ashford and Rye, with the Blenheim heading a bit west of south, the time came to bale out, but our troubles, mine particularly, were not over. I told Stride to go, which he did with a cheery 'See you both soon', but, just after Farrow followed when he saw Stride was safely out, there was a muffled explosion and a burst of flame fanned out immediately behind my seat. I had intended to delay following Farrow to make a last check that the Blenheim was heading safely out to sea, but the fire changed my mind for me. I released my seat harness, dived for the open hatch in the floor through which Farrow had left, but was pulled up with a jerk on my head. In a moment of panic I thought I was trapped with the flames spreading near me, but with a flood of relief I realised that I had forgotten to unplug my intercom lead. I put that right, hauled myself through the hatch, counted five and pulled the rip-cord. For a moment I remembered the scorched thigh straps, but there was a reassuringly strong tug from them as the canopy opened.

The sound of the slowly burning Blenheim died away quickly, and, as we heard no more of it, we assumed it ended up safely in the sea. The peace of the early morning sunshine was a benison, and it was so quiet that I could hear two lorries changing gear as they climbed the hill out of Rye. The three of us were drifting gently down, I suppose about 200 yards apart, along the line of the Blenheim's flight path, Farrow below me and Stride below him. I heard Farrow talking to Stride, whose reply I could not hear, and called, 'Are you two all right?'

I saw Farrow swing round to look up at me, throw up his arm pointing, and heard his anguished shout. 'God Almighty! Look at your canopy!' I looked up, saw a small circle of fire near the top of my canopy above my right shoulder, and with a sickening stab of fright realised I had not escaped safely from the burning Blenheim after all. Unless I reached the ground pretty quickly, I was going to do so with little help from my parachute. Some idle crew-room chat one day about someone in the same predicament came to my rescue; with both hands I grabbed the shroud-lines on my left and pulled down as hard as I could. For a moment I thought nothing was happening, but then the air spilled out of most of my canopy.

I started descending rapidly, slanting down underneath first Farrow and then Stride. Both were saying something to me, but I did not listen. I was too busy watching the widening hole in my canopy, and the ground coming up to me. I had to delay checking my descent as long as it was safe to do so, but how long was safe? A passage from a Victorian novel, probably by G. A. Henty, 'Don't shoot until you see the whites of their eyes', flashed incongruously across my mind.

I watched a hedge round a cornfield and, when the details suddenly became alarmingly clear, I let go of the shroud-line and the canopy filled. I felt the jerk on my harness as my descent was checked, saw the now much larger burning hole, grabbed the shroud-line webbing on each side, intending to give a heave upwards just before I hit the ground. I was too late; the ground hit me. A shock of pain shot through my whole body and bars of light flashed across my eyes, as I landed, cartwheeled over, and became entangled in my shroud-lines. I lay winded and stunned for a few moments before the smell of smouldering parachute silk revived me. In a daze I groped for the release buckle of my parachute harness, turned it, thumped it, and rolled away as the harness dropped free. I stood up shakily and heard the report of a shot-gun. Someone shouted, 'Lie down, you bastard, or I'll fire at you next time.'

Nothing loath, I lay down on my back in the young corn, enjoying the feel of the sun on my face, eyes closed, enjoying being alive and seemingly not badly hurt. I could not work out why I had been shouted at so rudely, but I did not care much, happy to let events flow over me. They did.

I felt someone toeing me and looked up to see a man in a cap and tweed jacket pointing his 12-bore at me, and two others, looking like young farm labourers, holding pitchforks at the ready. 'Right then. Don't move,' said Cap and Tweed Jacket. 'Who are you?'

'I'm an RAF Flying Officer,' I said meekly, pointing to the rank braid on the shoulders of my black overall jacket and my pilot's brevet. As I answered one of the labourers was stamping on the remains of my canopy, the fire having been merely smothered by the unburned folds.

'How do I know you're not a German parachutist or an agent in disguise? Tell me that.' Cap and Tweed Jacket prodded me with his foot again.

Muddled and dazed as I was, it was not until afterwards that it occurred to me to wonder why he thought a parachutist or an agent would be arriving unarmed and on fire in broad daylight. I was wondering how I was going to identify myself when a shout came from over the hedge to save me. 'It's all right, Father. He's RAF. The two sergeants of a Blenheim crew are with me and they want to know how their pilot is. He must have hit the ground with a hell of a smack.'

The atmosphere changed completely. The pitchforks were stuck in the ground, and I was helped to my feet. 'Sorry about that, my boy,' said Cap and Tweed Jacket with his shot-gun over the crook of his arm, 'but I had to make sure. We'll go to the farmhouse and my wife will look after you.' One of the labourers bundled up the remains of my parachute. With the other labourer and Cap and Tweed Jacket taking one of my arms each, we crossed the field to a road where Farrow and Stride, accompanied by Cap and Tweed Jacket's son and several others, were smiling at me in relief, and saying how pleased they were I had been so lucky to survive my burning descent.

Cap and Tweed Jacket explained that they were Local Defence Volunteers. I had heard of them being formed, but had never thought of being involved with them. They shortly afterwards became the Home Guard.

In the farmhouse we were given tea with bacon and eggs and most kindly treated while we waited for a car which Farrow's telephone call to Hawkinge had summoned. At Hawkinge I was given a thorough check by the medical officer, who took some convincing I had not broken any bones or was not concussed. Without telling me what it was, the MO gave me a drink which put me to sleep for six hours. When I woke I went hungry to the mess for dinner. The squadron had been hard at it all day. Jasper Johns and two others, who had been in our pub party the two evenings before, had been killed together with their crews. A fourth was missing and later reported captured.

On 31 May we did three more bombing sorties in a newly delivered aircraft, successfully we thought. Apart from meeting occasional bursts of ack-ack fire which did only superficial damage, the sorties were uneventful, and set us off early in the morning of 1 June full of confidence for yet another bombing sortie.

The reports of the bitter anger in the BEF against us were increasing in volume, and there were unpleasant scenes at Channel ports with returning soldiers insulting anyone in RAF uniform. Accordingly, we were told that, when we had dropped our bombs, we should fly low over the Dunkirk beaches and let the soldiers see us. I was not at all anxious to do any such thing. One reason why we had survived the day before so successfully was that we had made our approaches to the targets so that we kept away from trouble as long as possible, and had always taken the safest route home as soon as our bombs had gone. The safest route home was well away from the battle zone, but ours was not to reason why...

Up to this morning we had been attacking targets east of Nieuwpoort, but our targets today were well west and south-west of Nieuwpoort as the Germans followed the contracting perimeter. We dropped our bombs and, following our instructions, I pushed the nose down so that when I reached the British positions I was flying along at about 50 feet over the crowded beaches waggling my wings. Stride was waving from his gun turret. Suddenly, from directly in front of me came a heavy, no-deflection burst of Bren-gun fire, and a solid stream of bullets thumped into my starboard engine. There was instantaneously a belch of thick black smoke and an explosion of flame. All I could do was to slam my throttles shut and shove the nose of the Blenheim onto the sand straight ahead. Through the billows of smoke I could see soldiers fanning out from in front of me. Farrow had already opened the hatch above me as we ground to a jagged stop, and immediately pulled himself out. I followed him as quickly as I could onto the port wing and jumped from it onto the sand, straight into the arms of a Roman Catholic padre in his surplice.

He grabbed my hand and together we dashed up the beach with ammunition and petrol exploding around us. We flopped down panting behind a shallow fold in the sand.

'My word!' he said between gasps. 'I never believed the Holy Ghost could be scattered so quickly.' He had been celebrating Mass, and I had landed right on top of the hinged box containing his chalice and wine, which he used as a portable altar. 'What happened to you? You appeared from nowhere.'

The Blenheim ammunition was still exploding and the blaze flared up and died down as successive fuel tanks caught fire, but, sheltered by our ridge of sand, we were able to carry on a conversation with our faces close to the sand. I explained why we had been told to fly low along the beach after our bombing attack. The padre told me that his brigade was expecting to be embarked at any moment and that we should not be on the beach long. 'Which is just as well after the ungrateful way someone along there has treated you,' he added grinning, and pointing back the way I had come.

As the funeral pyre of my poor Blenheim died down, we were joined by Farrow and Stride, and soldiers who had been befriending them. At first these soldiers had not been too friendly, but Stride, who had a powerful turn of speech when roused, had quickly told them what he thought of being shot down by one of them. 'We have plenty of casualties coping with the bloody Germans trying to help you without you lot joining in against us.'

Because of his forthright words, we became the centre of an interested circle with whom we and our padre were soon swapping battle stories. All this time German bombs and shells were exploding intermittently near and far on the beach, but, in spite of the seemingly crowded conditions, the troops were so arranged in thin lines that there was much unoccupied sand. Casualties were surprisingly few.

Our padre had arranged, miraculously it seemed to me, for mugs of tea and we were enjoying them, Farrow and Stride handing out cigarettes, when a sergeant and five soldiers of the Northumberland Fusiliers came running up. They were shouting excitedly that the Germans they had shot down were their prisoners and they wanted them. When they saw us, and realised what had happened, the change of expression on their Northumbrian faces was farcical. Our soldiers made derisive remarks, giggling, while Farrow and I did not stop drinking our tea. Stride, with his usual Canadian succinctness, said over his shoulder 'Oh, piss off!' and they did.

Shortly afterwards, our unit was given orders to make their way out to a tug-boat, the *Isle of Thanet*, which was standing off-shore with barges in tow. During the embarkation we had been separated from the padre and our other friends. We found ourselves in a barge with an unfriendly lot who eyed us askance when they took any notice of us, and seemed to feel we should have been left on the beach. Farrow and Stride muttered furiously about them, but I was too weary of their attitude to care. It was a long, embarrassing journey across the Channel and up the Thames Estuary to Sheerness, where the ritual cheers for the navy and the boos for us took place as we disembarked. Some RAF policemen on the jetty took us to their temporary base, a garage, until a car arrived to take us to Hawkinge.

When I was on my way to report to the Operations Room after an early breakfast the next day, 2 June, the squadron commander overtook me in his car. He stopped and spoke to me through his window as I saluted him.

Alastair, we are being taken out of the line while we get some new aircrew and aircraft lined up. I don't need you for a bit, so nip off back to your aunt's for a few days. We'll recall you if we need you, but I doubt if we shall. It seems that the evacuation from the beaches is not likely to last for more than another two or three days.

'Are you sure, sir, there's nothing I can do?' I made the ritual offer with little fervour, as he knew full well.

'I'm sure,' he said grinning. 'Don't push your luck by asking, or I might take you up on your offer! The adjutant is arranging leave for your crew as well.'

I went back to the officers' mess and packed a suitcase. Then, when I was in the adjutant's office to sign the leave book and collect a railway warrant, the squadron commander opened the door to his adjoining office.

'Alastair,' he said, looking at the railway warrant in my hand, 'you'll only need the return half of that. I've arranged for you to be flown up to Dyce.' Dyce was a fairly new airfield about 6 miles north-west of Aberdeen. 'One of the new crews have never flown together before and I'm sending them off on a long navigation exercise to settle them down by getting to know each other. Don't worry!' he added, amused by an expression of misgiving which must have passed over my face. 'Although the navigator and air-gunner are straight out of training school, the pilot has been instructing on Blenheims. You'll be safe with him!'

A beaming Aunt Bessie was waiting for me at Dyce, having been warned of my arrival time by the Hawkinge Operations Room. Within twenty-four hours of drinking tea with the padre on the beach at Dunkirk, I was having a late lunch with her at Craigwell.

After this lunch we had coffee in deck-chairs in the garden and Aunt Bessie dozed off. Alone with my thoughts, I found myself wanting to find a way to define the sharply changing feelings and emotions brought about by the sudden changes of fortune I had met in the flying operations of the past few days. I would leave orderly civilised circumstances, and within a very short time be in a situation of chaotic discomfort and danger, and vice versa. From my musings, I evolved the idea of a Contrasting Feelings Factor, or CFF for short.

Drinking tea with the padre on the beach at Dunkirk and having coffee with Aunt Bessie in the

garden at Craigwell was an example of CFF. So was
wandering round the elegant chateau near Louvain,
marked and singed from my encounter with the six
ME 109s; so was enjoying the peace of the village pub
at Hawkinge after a day's operating over the battle
area; and so was baling out between Ashford and Rye,
being threatened by Cap and Tweed Jacket, and then
having bacon and eggs at the farmhouse. Some years
later an Australian fighter pilot was telling me how
he had been captured after his aircraft had exploded.
'There I was a bloody prisoner, still sucking my bloody
breakfast off my bloody back teeth.' He was experien-
cing a case of CFF.

For two days I spent most of my time in the garden
enjoying the peace and the lovely weather, reading a
good deal, doing odd jobs in the garden, and helping
Aunt Bessie in her many local activities when I experienced a discordant episode.

Aunt Bessie had to drive into Kintore to collect
some medical supplies for Donald Malcolm's surgery
and to do some shopping. I went to keep her company.

While I was waiting for her outside a shop, I saw, on the other side of the street, a TA gunner lieutenant with his mother, a friend of Aunt Bessie. He and I were the same age, and had played tennis and golf together in school holidays. As I saw them first I called out, 'Hullo, Kenneth, delighted to see you back safely!'

He turned, saw me, and his expression darkened. 'No thanks to your lot,' he sneered. 'I suppose you've been on leave the whole time.'

'Oh, Kenneth, don't say such things.' His mother put a hand on his arm, and gave me an alarmed look; she had heard something of what had been happening to me. 'Alastair has been in lots of trouble.'

'Don't worry.' I gave her a wan smile. 'I'm used to this sort of thing now, unfortunately.' I gave him a firm, but bowdlerised, version of Stride's outburst on the beach three days before.

Kenneth gaped at me, crestfallen. 'I'm sorry, I'd no idea.'

'No,' I replied bitterly, thinking of Jasper, Christie, Bence, and the many others. 'I don't suppose you had. You and the rest of them.'

Kenneth's mother had been looking more and more distressed, knowing he had upset me, whispering 'Oh dear! Oh dear!' quietly at intervals. I wanted to say something kind to her, and fortunately I was able to thank her and say how much the WVS help she was giving to Aunt Bessie was appreciated.

On 5 June, when the Prime Minister declared that the Evacuation of Dunkirk was officially over, he used the opportunity to praise the work of the Royal Air Force. I felt guilty about my malicious satisfaction as I hoped Kenneth had heard it.

Map of Dunkirk showing the area along the coast where the evacuation of the British Expeditionary Force took place between 27 May and 4 June, 1940.

Map kindly sourced and supplied by the Research Department at RAF Hendon.

CHAPTER 4

BACK TO BATTLE

When I woke on the morning of 3 June, I felt a glow of relief that the Dunkirk evacuation must be nearly over. I hoped, and felt guilty about the craven hope, that my squadron commander would not have to change his mind about needing me; having unwound for three days, I was in no hurry for the unwinding process to come to an end. Then, in the middle of the morning, the squadron adjutant ended my leave by telephone. I was called in from trying to do the *Scotsman* crossword puzzle in the garden at Craigwell to hear him say, 'Sorry to have to bring you back, Alastair, but the CO is having to send you to France tomorrow morning to take over our detached recce flight. We've just heard that the flight commander and his crew were killed yesterday.'

While I was making my way back from being shot down in Belgium on 11 May, a small reconnaissance flight of three Blenheims had been detached from 53 Squadron and sent to France to operate directly under our Commander-in-Chief's HQ, which controlled the fighter and bomber squadrons based in the area around Rheims, 70 miles east of Paris. It was the commander of this flight whom I was replacing.

'The CO', continued the adjutant, 'wants to see you before you leave to brief you about the job. He would like to have lunch with you tomorrow in the mess. Can you make it all right?'

'Surely,' I replied, trying not to feel anything. Although there seemed interesting possibilities in a detached reconnaissance flight, I did not feel at all brave, and wanted to stay where I was, wrapped in the peace of the Aberdeenshire countryside.

'By the way,' the adjutant went on, 'I'm glad to be the first to congratulate you. Your promotion to acting flight lieutenant has just come in from Group Headquarters.'

'Oh, good!' I replied, feeling a little more war-like now. I had not expected anything like that.

'Dead man's shoes, old boy,' the adjutant chuckled. 'Incidentally, the squadron has moved to Eastchurch. See you there, properly dressed, I hope.' He chuckled again.

'Thank you for telling me about Eastchurch,' I said

in a flat voice, trying not to sound too sarcastic. 'You've saved me from hurrying off to Hawkinge.'

'Not at all, old boy,' he replied, still chuckling and rang off. I looked at the telephone as I replaced the receiver; he need not have said that about dead man's shoes for he was running little risk, in the administrative branch, of being one of the dead men; also, there seemed to be little chance of my being 'properly dressed'; his facetious remark referred to the tailoring addition of a second piece of rank braid on my tunic to show I was a flight lieutenant. He knew full well there was little time for me to have it done. 'Damn him!' I thought. 'If I can possibly have it done, I shall. I'll show him!'

Even with this thought came another. Why was I being so petty in my attitude to this dug-out from the last war? Had he not been fighting for us before I was born? Was it his fault he was now in his mid-forties, tall, plumpish, good-looking, and very well-off by our standards? If he was so often boring us with stories starting 'When I was on Camels' it was probably because he was trying to be one of the boys. If he grated on me, was it not because I was on edge, envying him for his security? I hoped I had not revealed my feelings to him, and resolved to be on my guard to keep them to myself.

I telephoned Aberdeen station, learned an overnight train was leaving for King's Cross which I should be able to catch, and that I should have to go to Charing Cross for a train to Eastchurch on the Isle of Sheppey. Aunt Bessie drove me into Aberdeen with just enough time to call in to say goodbye to Donald Malcolm at his surgery, and I was on my way back to war. Always on these departures my courage was at a low ebb. Sitting in the train alone with my thoughts, foreboding trembling in my stomach, I was very conscious of the trouble in loved eyes and the faint tremble of lips which covered the unsaid words and belied the banal expressions of departure. Standing by the open window of my carriage as the train started to pull out, Aunt Bessie had said, 'Try not to take risks,' and then looked embarrassed by the futility of what she had said.

I knew my despondency would pass as soon as I had something to do, but until then I was so unsettled that I avoided facing my feelings.

I went straight to Charing Cross from King's Cross on the advice of the Aberdeen station-master. He had

said that, as the Southern Railway was still very busy
with troop movements from the Channel ports in
the aftermath of Dunkirk, it was better to ask at the
station for a train to Eastchurch rather than rely on
timetables. At Charing Cross, finding that I had two
and a half hours to wait, I thought I would try Moss
Brothers in Covent Garden to see if they would alter
my rank braid, but found that it would be easier to buy
a complete uniform. I was wandering slowly down
the Strand in the sunshine, not feeling hungry and
wondering what to do to fill in time, when I saw a small
shop selling ribbons, laces and buttons with a notice
in the window 'Military Repairs Carried Out'. In I
went, and was greeted with a beaming smile from the
firmly plump, adenoidal elderly Jewess behind
the counter.

'Come in, my dear! What can I do to help you?'

'I need another strip of rank braid on my sleeve,'
I said, holding out my left arm and suddenly feeling
bashful. 'But I have a train to catch at 5.30.'

'No trouble, my dear. Pleased to do it for you.' The
lady's smile broadened. 'Just been promoted, eh? Well
done! Come into the room at the back, dear, where I
have a machine, and give me your tunic.'

'I'm afraid the one stripe will have to be moved up or down before the second is added,' I explained diffidently.

'Oh! I know all about that,' she said. 'Let me start!'

While she worked, I sat behind the counter in my shirt-sleeves, and found myself serving customers, helped by advice called out to me above the clatter of the sewing machine. It was fun and my nervous queasiness vanished with my depression into the background. Did this qualify, I wondered smiling at myself, as yet another case of CFF that I should be celebrating my promotion by serving in a small haberdashery in the Strand?

When my tunic was ready, there was still time to spare. I slipped out and bought biscuits and cake from a nearby Lyons, which my benefactress and I ate together with the tea which she brewed on a gas ring. Relaxed by her kindness, I was able to enjoy my slow journey through Kent to Eastchurch, happily continuing to read Galsworthy's Forsyte Saga. I had started reading it in the sick quarters at Tangmere on 21 May while I was waiting for the MO to examine me.

After dinner in the mess at Eastchurch, following a drink in the bar to celebrate my promotion, my story of the shop in the Strand being the subject of much hilarious disbelief, the squadron commander sent me down to the Operations Room, saying he would be along shortly. There, to my relief and pleasure I found Farrow and Stride waiting for me. Their faces lighted up, mirroring my feelings.

'Oh! I am so glad to see you,' I said, shaking their hands in turn. 'I was afraid we might be separated.'

'So were we, sir!' Farrow and Stride chimed in together. 'We didn't trust the reorganisation we'd heard was going on,' Farrow added.

'And congratulations on the promotion, sir!' Stride was beaming. 'The whole squadron is delighted.' It was very encouraging and warming to find they were as pleased to be with me as I was to be with them.

The squadron commander joined us, saying, 'It is good to see you three together again. Carry on with the good work. There's plenty to do. And that's a massive understatement.' He picked up his personal pointer, an old brassie less its club head, and pointed to the map hanging behind the low dais on which he stood.

This is the position. General Weygand has assumed command of the French army in the field, and the so-called Weygand Line has been formed along the south side of the Somme and eastwards to link up with the north end of the Maginot Line in Alsace. After Dunkirk, the German army has been regrouping and has started attacking this line at Abbeville, Amiens and Peronne, here, here, and here.

He pointed out the three positions. 'In support of this line are our Hurricanes, Battles and Blenheims under our Commander-in-Chief. Although they have had heavy casualties, these squadrons are still operating from their bases in the general area around Rheims, here, in support of the French Army.'

He again pointed with the tip of his brassie shaft.

Their supply base is here, the port of St Nazaire, near Nantes. Our C-in-C has found out that, in the confusion which has arisen out of the successive catastrophic defeats of the French army, he has been receiving less and less reliable information. To plug this intelligence gap is the purpose of our detached flight of three Blenheims, which is currently here at Coulommiers.

He pointed to a position some 35 miles east of the middle of Paris. 'Your task is to provide constant reports of the German advanced positions.' He paused and looked firmly at all three of us in turn. 'And nothing else! No heroic offensive action! Keep out of trouble as much as possible and only fire your guns in self-defence. As far as I know, there are no bombs at Coulommiers, and if there are,' he paused and smiled at us in turn, 'have nothing to do with them! You will be given orders by army liaison officers attached to our Headquarters. I'm sure they will agree with me about the offensive action; they know only too well how much they are relying on the information you bring them.'

The squadron commander paused for a drink of water.

Well, there you are. What living conditions will be like I do not know, but take camp kit with you. I've arranged a package of food as emergency rations for yourselves. Keep it intact in the aircraft as long as you can. The accountant officer is arranging an imprest account of 10,000 francs for your flight for any essential needs. Keep in touch with me as far as you can to let me know what is happening. You'll be on your own.

I don't know if you have heard, Alastair, but the 51st Highland Division with your brother Colin's battalion is on the west flank of the Weygand Line. They were brought across from their detachment to the Maginot Line after 10 May to be part of the French 10th Army.

'I had heard when I was at my aunt's', I said, 'that they were back from the Maginot, but I didn't know where.'

'Well, I guess you will be operating over them. I hope for your sake, as well as for all of us, that you will be able to report some encouraging news. I'll be thinking of you and your anxiety about your brother.' He clipped his make-shift pointer to the side of the small lectern, collected his papers together from the top of it, smiled at all three of us in turn, and left saying 'Good luck!'

I sent Farrow and Stride off to find the duty ground crew and to arrange to have our aircraft ready for an 06.30 take-off. When they had done that they were to draw three sets of camp kit, including sleeping bags, if possible, from stores and have them stowed in our Blenheim, together with the rations the squadron commander had mentioned. Then I had a flash of foresight.

'Also, if you can scrounge it, get hold of a large heavy-based saucepan. If we have to do our own cooking, it will be multi-purpose.'

'Yes, sir,' Stride came alight with pleasure at the prospect. 'I know what to look for. It'll be just the job for my corned-beef hash!' He was the first Canadian I had met, but by no means the last, who felt he had a mission in life to make corned-beef hash.

Anxious to lay my hands on the 10,000 francs, I went off to find the accountant officer and caught him just as he was going to bed. With great good humour he went to his office, drew the money out of his safe, and gave me a form on which to record my expenditure, explaining what I had to do. Then, guessing I was not paying very close attention, and indeed I was not, he laughed and said in a most unaccountant-officer-like way, 'Well, there you are. That's what you are supposed to do, but, when the time comes, we'll fudge something up if you have been in difficulties.'

'Such as losing the form, or my fountain pen, or being shot down,' I grinned.

In the hangar which housed the duty ground crew, I found Farrow and Stride, who told me delightedly how helpful everyone had been. Stride showed me with great pride a heavy frying pan and an equally heavy saucepan. We then went to the Navigation Office and drew a selection of maps to cover the general area from the Somme to the Loire. I left them with Farrow to arrange them in a convenient order with Stride's help, and went to bed. It seemed a long time since I had been summoned to the telephone from my crossword puzzle in the garden at Craigwell.

The newly arranged transport route to France was now from Warmwell, near Weymouth in Dorset, to Cherbourg, reflecting the German advances in north France.

By 07.30 the next day, 5 June, we were flying at 2,000 feet in mid-Channel in the bright sunshine which we were now accepting as commonplace in that lovely, disastrous summer. We completed an uneventful flight round Paris to the south, and landed on the small grass airfield at Coulommiers. Normally the grass on airfields was kept short, but, not surprisingly I supposed, it had not been cut for some time, and our airscrews fanned the foot-long grass flat. I taxied gingerly over it, worried about hidden obstacles, towards the only visible building, a small barn, which had an RAF ensign flying from a make-shift flag-pole outside.

CHAPTER 5

COULOMMIERS

I was delighted to see an old friend, Sergeant Hallows, emerge from the end of the barn, grinning and waving. He was the hero of the journey on a tractor, towing a petrol-bowser from Poix to Boulogne. I knew that our flight of three Blenheims had a ground party thirteen strong attached to it, but in the short time at Eastchurch I had not gathered their names. If I had been asked to pick a sergeant to be in charge of the ground crew, I would have asked for Hallows. When I joined 53 Squadron at Odiham from Cranwell in January 1938, Hallows was a corporal recently returned from a five-year tour on the North-West Frontier of India. He had been in charge of the servicing of my aircraft; we had both played together in the Odiham cricket team; I had been a guest at his wedding at the end of 1938; and, as a very inexperienced pilot officer, I had learned much from him.

Hallows directed me to where he wanted me to park, and I switched off the engines on his signal. He then jumped up onto the wing beside me, and when I opened the hatch I called out, 'Delighted to see you.'

'And you too, sir.' He beamed, looking down on me. 'We were wondering whom we were going to get. Have you been promoted?'

'Yes.' I grinned up at him with the warm feeling of relief to be welcomed like this by someone I knew so well.

'Great stuff!' he replied. 'Thank God something's been done right in all this shambles!' When Farrow and Stride joined us on the grass, I introduced them to Hallows, who had not met them. He had already been sent back to France before they joined the squadron.

'Do you play dominoes?' he asked them. 'If you don't, we'll teach you. We're great on dominoes in the sergeants' mess. In the officers' mess, as there are only three of them, they are always looking for a fourth at bridge from us or from the airmen's mess.'

'Sergeants' mess? Officers' mess? Airmen's mess? That all sounds very GS.' I smiled, puzzled. 'I thought we would be living pretty rough.'

'GS' stood for 'General Service', a term applied to

many items of equipment from boots upwards, and in our slang it stood for anything which conformed to regulations. Hallows laughed. 'Well, it sounds pukka enough, but in fact the three messes are only three different-sized tables in one room upstairs in the village cafe, one for the officers, one for the six aircrew sergeants and myself, and one for the two corporals and ten erks.'

Hallows went on to explain that an arrangement had been made with the cafe proprietor and his wife, Monsieur and Madame Montaigne, that they were given our rations from which they produced two meals a day, breakfast and supper, and a sandwich lunch. With all our flights they were a very popular pair who went out of their way to be helpful; all we did towards the feeding was to help with the washing-up. The cafe was about 200 yards down the secondary road which ran past the airfield. We slept in the tents I could see beyond the barn, which served as a flight office, work-shop and store-room.

Hallows saw me looking at two airmen who were standing near the far end of the barn watching us. They had rifles slung over their shoulders. An anxious look came over Hallows' face. 'We always keep two armed airmen on guard, day and night. It's the refugees. They'll steal anything, petrol, food, clothes, and some of them are pretty ugly buggers too. Deserters many of them, I wouldn't be surprised.'

'You've said rations are delivered daily. What about petrol? Do we get 100 octane?' I asked.

'There is plenty in underground tanks. We have to pump it up by hand. It's a bit suspect so we strain it through chammy leather. It's a slow business, refuelling.'

'What about police?' I asked.

'Never seen one in the ten days I've been here, sir. Apart from the Montaignes, no one does anything for us. Very few even smile at us. Even the Montaignes have to let it be known that they have been forced to help us.' Irritated, Hallows kicked at a tuft of grass.

Remembering the attitude of the people I had met on the hospital train journey from Brussels and in the village at Crécy, I was not surprised. As Hallows finished speaking, I saw through the trees a refugee car, with the familiar mattress topping, stop. Two figures alighted from it and came towards us through the trees; they were carrying heavy walking sticks. One of the two guards, with his rifle slung from his shoulder, came from behind the barn and intercepted them. '*Que voulez-vous?*' he asked politely.

The two stopped, looked round in a calculating and surly manner, returned the way they had come and, without a word, drove away.

'That's typical,' Hallows grunted. 'It's happening all the time. If we didn't keep our fingers well out, we'd lose the lot.' This incident set the pattern with which I was going to become very familiar in the ensuing days, and which indeed I came to accept as a matter of course.

The few days which followed our arrival at Coulommiers were quite unlike any other experience I had had before or have had since. Provided we never relaxed our basic precautions, it was a curiously trouble-free, uncomplicated existence; we learned that it was safer to expect everyone's hand to be against us, which added spice to the pleasure of being in a hard-working and disciplined unit, isolated from the leaderless, disintegrating atmosphere around us. Whatever was to happen, we all knew that the circumstances in which we found ourselves could only be short-lived, and everyone instinctively felt they could give of their best without stint. Our task was simple: we were asked to carry out six sorties a day, two by each aircraft, and to provide the backing to achieve them. For the first time I was answerable to no one as to how the work was done, and we improvised as we went along.

The jobs that had to be done by everybody were obvious to everybody. During the day time, those who were temporarily out of a job took their ease in the sunshine on the grass, and there always seemed to be at least two airmen kicking a football at each other. When work for the day was over, usually by about seven-thirty, we were all able to relax, apart from the two guards. In our room in the cafe at Coulommiers the darts board and the tennis table were usually in use against a background of clacking dominoes and quiet calls from the bridge players. I finished the Forsyte Saga there, and started on Hugh Walpole's London series.

We were living from day to day and enjoying each day as it came. I had some feelings of guilt, but not many and not deep, about our relatively carefree life.

The future for France looked grim, not only because of the Germans, but also because of the hopeless attitude of the French themselves. Although we did not need to be reminded that my predecessor and his crew had been killed, there was nothing to be gained by worrying.

At midday, the other two Blenheims of our flight returned from their sorties, and I met the crews, who were both new to me. Like their late flight commander, they had joined the squadron and been sent to Coulommiers in my absence. The two pilots were both pilot officers on their first operational postings; Raymond Chancery was a 28-year-old Oxford graduate who had just qualified as a chartered accountant when, as an RAF Volunteer Reserve pilot, he was called up on the outbreak of war; and Peter Holmes, a New Zealander of twenty, had just started his training as a short service commission officer when the war started. They both had a lively sense of humour, and I immediately found them to be very good company. I felt very lucky to have them.

Both Chancery and Holmes had little of note to report in their areas along the Weygand Line. One interesting feature of our task in keeping a check on German movements was that it was not enough to report that no movement was seen. We had to be as sure as we could that the Germans were or were not present in any particular area. This often entailed flying very low, particularly over wooded areas, and in fact all our flying was at low level in what, for all practical purposes, were ground level temperatures. In the continuous fine weather the cabin temperatures made for hot, sticky work.

On that first afternoon I and my crew spent a longer than usual time in the air to make up for the sortie missed in the morning. We were covering the area south of the Somme and the Oise from Abbeville to Soissons. We could see considerable signs of activity, but no signs of German penetration. Refugees in plenty we saw and allied military traffic, mostly French, to and from the line, but no Germans. We had covered the area twice and had begun to think that the French 10th Army, which included our 51st Highland Division, were holding the German attacks. Then, flying towards the sea in a westerly direction for the third time, we saw, with a kind of dismay, that the Germans had broken through near Péronne and Abbeville.

The routine arrangement was that one or other of two Army liaison officers at Headquarters called on us early in the morning to give us our tasks for the day, and in the early evening they called again to collect our information. On this evening when I landed, a Major Jameson was already there, talking to Chancery and Holmes, who had been flying to the east of my area. They were looking cheerful and laughing together, and I guessed rightly that they had had no penetrations to report. My two pilots had already told me how easy it was to work with Major Jameson. He greeted me in a most friendly manner, but my news sobered him immediately.

'You are absolutely sure of this, are you?' he asked frowning, when I pointed out the German positions, and questioned Farrow and me closely about the details of what we had seen. He told us to cover the same areas the next day, quickly finished the mug of coffee which Hallows had produced for him, apologised to me for not staying to have what he called a 'hullo chat', and left on his motorbike. He found it the best, if not the most comfortable, vehicle for dealing with the congested roads.

While Sergeant Hallows and his men were preparing the aircraft for the next day, I took Farrow and Stride off to a small river nearby where Chancery and Holmes and their crews were already swimming. In the hot weather I usually wore a Cranwell physical training vest, what we would now call a T-shirt, in heavy cotton, trimmed at the neck and sleeves in pale blue, and navy blue running shorts under the squadron two-piece black flying overalls. I much amused the others by going naked into the water, soaping myself all over, and having a rinse. Then I put on my swimming shorts and washed my socks, vest, shorts and overalls before having a swim. Whenever I could I did the same thing each evening while we were in France, and only twice did I have to make do with a bucket of water. With no normal facilities available to us, life had to be reduced to simple, practical terms; one result was that I never unpacked my uniform out of my suitcase, which remained in the Blenheim. In spite of my being laughed at the first time I washed myself, my soap was soon much in demand, and my alfresco example of personal hygiene soon became routine among the aircrew.

That evening after a remarkably good meal in the cafe of vegetable soup, omelette and bully-beef fritters, the Montaignes asked me into their sitting room for coffee and cognac. They were clearly very worried. The postal system had stuttered to a halt, and they had given up trying to speak by telephone to their daughter in Rheims. Monsieur Montaigne had a large life assurance policy which had matured a few days before. The company was based in Arras and he had heard nothing from it. Remembering how, at the end of May, I had seen the BEF battling around Arras before withdrawing towards Dunkirk, I was not surprised. I could not comfort him about the possibility of seeing his money soon, if ever. When I thought of how many people all over north France must be suffering fearful uncertainties, if not disaster and bereavement, our little enclave on the airfield seemed to be enjoying a carefree idyll by comparison. Although we were taking part in the agony of France, we remained separate from it; England, peaceful and organised, awaited us across the Channel.

On our sortie the next morning we thought at first that the position had not changed significantly from the evening before. There was a certain amount of sporadic air activity, but no one, either in the air or on the ground, took much notice of us. Only a few token bursts of light anti-aircraft fire, easily dodged, came our way, and we pottered along with as many hatches open as possible to counter the heat of the sun. Then, a sharp shock of dismay shattered our peaceful progress; we saw a considerable German armoured force around Poix, 20 miles south of the Somme, the Poix where 53 Squadron had spent eight months up to May.

It was bad enough seeing the Germans there at all, but what was far worse was that they were clearly showing that they were meeting little opposition; the tanks were open with the crews basking in the sunshine; and a quick glance showed me that Madame Foullens' house was undamaged and there were no signs of battle in the rest of the village. I turned immediately towards Coulommiers, and hurried back to spread the bad news without delay.

Back at Coulommiers, while the aircraft was being refuelled and we were having coffee and cheese sandwiches, I explained to Sergeant Hallows what we had seen, and left him with marked maps in case Major Jameson appeared in our absence on the next sortie. With no telephones working and with no means of making our way to him, even if we knew where to go, we had to rely on him contacting us.

He appeared an hour or so after we had taken off, intending to wait for our return, but the news Hallows gave him sent him roaring away on his motorbike. He returned in the evening when we were swimming, and conducted a debriefing session on the river bank. As soon as we had reported some minor advances by the Germans, and he had taken note, I asked him, 'What news of the 51st? What are the plans for them?'

'We're hoping that they will be able to retreat to Le Havre and embark there, if necessary,' Jameson replied. 'But it depends on the French High Command organising the retreat so that the line to the right of the 51st is kept intact. You'll be worrying about your brother, I know.'

7 June 1940

The next morning the minor advances by the Germans we had reported the day before had become major ones. On our first sortie Farrow and I had more to cope with in our area over the west end of the line than we could record fully and accurately. Accordingly, on our return to Coulommiers, I left our inform-ation with Hallows as before, and divided my area with Chancery, leaving Holmes to deal on his own with the eastern end of the line where things were quieter.

I was anxious that any reconnaissance over the area around the 51st Division should be done by me. I would then be 1,000 feet above Colin. Although, for all the good I could do personally to help him, I might as well be 1,000 miles away, being there was my miserable best. I wondered unhappily if he might be watching my Blenheim with his binoculars, and seeing the large letters PZ-E, my aircraft identification letters, painted in white on each side of the fuselage; he knew them to be mine.

On my second sortie on that day, 7 June, Farrow and I saw the German advanced units were nearing Rouen and Beauvais, and watched their steady progress the day after. I had a most unhappy feeling that any chance of Colin with his division reaching Le Havre was very slim.

Early on the morning of 9 June I was told to pull out of Coulommiers and move to Chartres, some 40 miles south-west of Paris and about 90 miles away by road from where we were. The order, signed by a Squadron Leader Robinson, was delivered by a despatch rider. On the day before I had warned Sergeant Hallows that I thought we should have to move. In fact, he did not need much warning, being able to read the signs as well as anyone, and he had been preparing to travel. Although I had arranged to delay our three aircraft from taking off until he was ready, we did not have to wait long. Our plan was that he would drive the 3-tonner with the ground crew to Chartres and be there to meet us when we landed at the end of our second sorties. We took off twenty minutes after he left. I circled round and spotted him on the ominously crowded road; he had not gone very far.

All our three aircraft returned to a deserted Coulommiers. As we had to refuel ourselves by hand-pumping, we only took on board as much as we needed for three hours' flying instead of filling to capacity as was the usual procedure. I was anxious not to overtax the aircrew in the heat, and when the refuelling was finished and we had had something to eat, I ordered an hour's rest before taking off on the second sortie. During this hour I slipped down to the cafe to say farewell to the Montaignes; she was in tears and he was pale with worry. Whatever slight hopes they had had were killed by the remorseless German advance. I could bring them no comfort, and was touched by their unselfish wishes for our safe return home.

I rejoined the other aircrew who were lying in the shade chattering quietly. In the background was the rumble of traffic, but around us the air was loud with the insect drone of summer. I was interested and pleased that they all shared a feeling of magic about the days at Coulommiers. Against all probability, we had plucked, out of the war, a few days of happiness in which all had gone smoothly without, as far as I could tell, a cross word from anybody. We had been busy and content. We had avoided serious thought of the future, but the magic had gone with the departure of the 3-tonner. The silence, which now replaced the bustle of activity centred on Sergeant Hallows, began to be uncanny and to thrust the uncertain future on us. We were all glad when take-off time arrived.

CHAPTER 6

CHARTRES –
MAINLY DOMESTICITY

When I flew over the airfield at Chartres, I could see Chancery's and Holmes' Blenheims near a small hangar, but it was disappointingly obvious that Hallows and party had not arrived, although they had been on the road for some eight hours by that time. As I taxied towards the hangar through the now familiar near-hayfield, I felt bored at the thought of refuelling the aircraft ourselves for the second time that day. This boredom was emphatically shared by Farrow and Stride on the intercom and by the other two crews when we joined them, but there was no avoiding the sweaty labour. After our partial refuelling at Coulommiers at midday we did not have a lot left in the tanks, and it was essential that we kept the aircraft ready to move at short notice. As Holmes had already found the fuel installation and the handles for operating the pumps, each crew dealt with its own aircraft in turn. While two of us heaved on the pump handle to much singing about Volga boatmen, the third held the nozzle with its chamois leather strainer into the petrol tanks on the aircraft.

Farrow, Stride and I refuelled our aircraft first, and then set off to wash in a stream we had pinpointed near the airfield as we circled round before landing. By this time we all had our washing gear handy. I kept mine in the rope-handled canvas bucket belonging to my camp kit, together with my change of under-clothes; even without the refuelling, six hours or so of low flying in the heat made the wash and change most welcome. Farrow had rigged up a washing line in the storage well of our Blenheim so that sometimes we were flying on our sorties together with our drying laundry when we had no one to keep an eye on it on the ground. The fine summer weather, however, was good drying weather, and we only had to take our damp clothing into the air with us on two occasions.

In the hangar were two taps, but no water came from them, and afterwards we learned that the local water supply had failed two days earlier, the water engineers having departed southwards, leaving the local people dependent on whatever water they could obtain from wells.

When we returned from our ablutions, the other two crews, having completed their refuelling, went off with their washing things, leaving us to keep watch. Although our airfield was called Chartres, it lay between Chartres and a small village on the edge of which it stood. I asked Chancery and Holmes to walk into the village on their way back from the stream to see if any cafe arrangements on the Coulommiers lines were possible. With nothing to do except wait, we were able to relax in the evening sunshine. I read my Walpole; Farrow pulled out a crossword puzzle book; and Stride just relaxed with his inevitable thin cigar.

After an hour we heard a car hooting on the road, which carried its endless stream of refugees within about 75 yards of our hangar, and an English voice shouting 'Ahoy! 53 Squadron!' Stride leaped to his feet and hurried through the fringe of trees between the road and the hangar. He returned shortly afterwards along a track, standing in triumph on the running board of a Royal Army Service Corps (RASC) lorry which had come to deliver our food rations, plus two 4-gallon jerry cans of water. I had been wondering what to do about eating and drinking. Hallows, I knew, had little left in his 3-tonner, and the emergency ration packs our squadron commander had arranged for us would not have gone far among our 22-strong party. In addition to our rations, the RASC corporal and his mate also had a crate of canned beer which he said Major Jameson had wangled from somewhere for us. We immediately opened five tins.

At the time, and even more so in retrospect, it seemed miraculous to me how, through all the constant movement, turmoil and uncertainty, food continued to be delivered to us, and petrol and oil were always available. Well done indeed, the RASC!

The RASC corporal finished his beer quickly. 'With the roads blocked as they are, I never know how long any journey is going to take,' he said, getting into his cab. 'Nor do I know where I am going to end up. Last night I got back to my depot to find a notice pinned to the door saying that we'd moved to Alençon, and I had to go there sharpish. The bloody Jerries are breaking through everywhere. I suppose the Frogs are still on our side, but I do wonder.'

Chancery and Holmes and their crews returned clean, but unsuccessful except for two flagons of *vin ordinaire*. With the water shortage no cafe proprietors would consider helping us. Indeed, they seemed glad of the excuse not to help us; the last proprietor's wife even advised us to go home and not make things worse for them by annoying the Germans.

At 21.30, when I was finding that worry about Hallows was beginning to make my mind stray away from Walpole's London, he arrived with his stiff, tired, hungry and thirsty party. The first thing he asked, bless him, was whether the aircraft needed attention.

'We've done the refuelling.' I smiled round at the airmen, who all grinned in relief. 'And now we'll refuel ourselves. We've beer and wine and the rations have been delivered.' Very soon we were busily enjoying a picnic of bully beef, bread, pickles, margarine, cheese, and cold baked beans. By the time the speed of eating was dying down, and one of the fitters had the spirit stove roaring so that strong tea with condensed milk and sugar was ready to be drunk out of tin mugs, darkness had fallen. I told Hallows to set the first guard detail and let the others get to bed. Bed was a euphemism; it was a question of everybody finding somewhere to doss down; most of the ground crew slept in the little hangar; Farrow stretched out on the floor of his navigating position in our Blenheim and Stride slept in the open between the wheels in my sleeping bag on a ground-sheet. Just as I was wriggling into my sleeping bag, Hallows, with a torch in one hand and towel and soap in the other, asked the way to our washing place in the stream. I noticed that there was only one airman with him.

Early the next morning, when all was ready for take-off and the three aircrews were sitting around on the grass waiting for a liaison officer to brief us, Hallows came to me looking, for him, diffident. 'I'm sorry to bother you, sir, but I wonder if you would speak to the men for me.'

'Of course! What do you want me to say?' I stood up and walked with him a few paces away from the others.

'Well,' Hallows smiled apologetically, 'some of the erks are beginning to pong a bit. I know washing isn't easy, but if you could give them a nudge, I'm sure it would help. They'd pay attention to you.'

'Certainly I will,' I said straightaway, and Hallows looked relieved. I think he was afraid I would tell him to go and be his own nanny. 'You are absolutely right to bring the matter up. At Coulommiers the facilities in the cafe were just about adequate, but here there are no domestic arrangements. What's more I guess we shall be on the move from now onwards, and that makes its own problems. Give me ten minutes to collect my thoughts, and then gather everyone around here.'

I went to my cockpit where I had various manuals and pamphlets in a briefcase and took out the blue, rexine-covered RAF Field Service Pocket-Book. I flipped through this book making jottings on a piece of white card. Five years later, after the war, I found this card in one of the pockets of the overalls I was wearing that day, and on it I had jotted a list:

Worsening Conditions
Clean/Healthy
Army No. 1
FFA
Shaving
P and S
Boil Water
Foot-rot/Socks

The scene which followed has remained sharply etched into my memory, partly because for the first time in my life I was speaking to others about their personal hygiene, and partly because of the strong feeling of responsibility for the men and of the fellowship I shared with them. Our little party of twenty-two was isolated, compact and disciplined in the surrounding chaos. The sense of isolation was intensified by the incessant rumble of traffic on the road 50 yards away where the refugees passed, wholly intent on their own affairs. Our three Blenheims were ready for flight. In front of them the ground crew stood in a curve facing me, Sergeant Hallows on the right with the two armed guards at each end. Before them were the aircrew dressed for flying. With the blue pocket-book in one hand and my card of jotted headings in the other, I started to speak.

'I have quite a bit to say, so sit down on the grass where you are.' When they were settled down except for the two sentries, all looking expectantly towards me, I continued, holding up the pocket-book. 'In here you will find all you need to look after a unit in the field. There is much good stuff in it, but it presupposes a unit in a much better-equipped and in a more static situation than we are. Nevertheless, many of its rules still apply. At Coulommiers we were well off. Last night will have taught you things are much more rugged here, and I imagine we shall have to keep moving. Conditions will not improve and will probably get worse.' I paused to open the pocket-book where my finger marked the place and quoted from it. 'You must go to some trouble to look after yourselves, to keep clean to keep healthy.'

In the army they talk about two forms of washing, and I want you to look on these two forms as the minimum required. The first is called 'Army Number One'. It consists of rolling up your shirt-sleeves, tucking a towel into the back of your shirt-collar, and washing your hands, neck and face. The second is called an FFA, which stands for feet, fork and armpits. If you are clever, you expose each area to be attacked in turn, but it is really much better to find somewhere once a day where you can strip off and wash all over. The weather is fine and warm and you won't catch pneumonia. Those of you who need to shave...

I paused and looked along the line. This raised a

laugh, as I intended. The hairier, older ones nudged the owners of smooth, young faces. 'Those of you who need to shave, shave once a day if you possibly can. So much for washing, now about relieving yourselves.' I held up the pocket-book.

This goes into elaborate detail about field latrines, but we can't manage them; and, with our small numbers and the frequent times I expect we shall have to move, we shall do without them. But if you want to have a pee, move off at least 50 yards from where we are working, eating and sleeping. And as for more serious relief, take one of the hand-mattocks, sometimes called entrenching tools, we have in the kit; wander off into the bushes; cut a little slice of turf; dig a small hole and drop into it; put the bog-paper on top; replace the divot; and stamp it down. Then rinse your hands. We have no means of looking after anyone who is sick. So, for your own personal sake, keep fit, only drink boiled water, and keep a little boiled water for washing your teeth. One last thing. Your feet. Treat them with great care. If the 3-tonner breaks down, if the aircraft go unserviceable, if we get separated for any reason, any of us may find ourselves walking to keep away from the Germans. Keep your feet clean and dry. Keep your socks clean. Examine your feet daily for foot-rot, and shove on some fungicidal cream out of the first-aid kit at the first suspicion of trouble. That's all. Good luck! Carry on please. Sergeant Hallows!

As my audience, who had paid me the closest attention in silence, scrambled to their feet and started dispersing, an amused voice behind me cried, 'Amen to that! I fully support all you have said.' I spun round, and there stood a steel-helmeted squadron leader who had arrived unbeknownst to me while I had been speaking. He looked at the pocket-book in my hand. 'I'm so glad to see someone making use of that excellent little manual. You must be Panton. I've come to brief you.' He held out his hand and shook mine.

I'm Robinson on the Ops Staff at Headquarters. Major Jameson's been called away. He asked me to say that he is sorry he was not able to tell you himself, but will be in touch if he gets the chance. We are working as closely together as we can, and swapping information. How are you all getting on? You seem to have your flight well organised, as Jameson said.

I replied, with a warm feeling of pleasure,

Everything's gone well enough so far, sir, but the margin of safety's pretty narrow. The aircraft keep going, but we can manage little more than daily servicing and very minor rectifications. If the 3-tonner breaks down, the next move separates us from our ground crew. As it is, last night they did not arrive here until after nine-thirty, by which time we had done the refuelling.

'The roads are pretty grim,' Squadron Leader Robinson commented, 'and will get worse, but you all seem in high spirits.' He looked smiling at an airman trying to do a handstand while two others taunted him.

'Oddly enough, sir, we are enjoying ourselves, living from day to day and hand to mouth, wondering how long the picnic's going to last.'

'Come over here with me.' Robinson, speaking in a low voice, walked away from the few others still remaining from our meeting.

You won't have to be a great strategist to realise everything's in the melting pot. I don't believe there's any chance of the French making much of a stand. There's some talk about forming a defensive line, a sort of 'Torres Vedras', across the foot of the Brittany peninsula, but I doubt if the Germans will let the position stabilise long enough for that to happen, even if there are enough troops available. It's my guess that you won't be needed in France for more than another week or so. We are falling back westwards so that Cherbourg, St Malo, Brest and St Nazaire will be available for evacuation. Meanwhile we need your daily reconnaissance reports urgently. In all the rumours and uncertainties your reports are accepted verbatim without reservation. We rely on them absolutely to know what is going on.

He then went on to give me our tasks for that day, which roughly covered a line from Le Havre in the west to Rheims and Metz in the east.

He had words of praise and encouragement with Chancery and Holmes and their crews, and had a mug of sweet, orange-coloured tea with Hallows. Then, saying that he would see us again that evening, he set off on his motorbike to check on the whereabouts and state of various retreating RAF units.

All our three Blenheims returned unscathed from our morning sorties, and to my pleased surprise I found a smiling, but worried-looking Major Jameson waiting for me. 'I happened to be passing. I've kept in touch with your movements through Robinson, and I'm here to learn what I can from you, particularly about the 51st Highlanders. I knew you, if anyone, would know. What's new?'

'Only gloom, I'm afraid,' I replied. 'I'm sure there's not the slightest chance of them reaching Le Havre. We've seen German tanks and armoured vehicles east of the 51st, between them and Le Havre, 10 miles from Fécamp.'

As I was speaking, Jameson was marking his map. 'I'm sure you're right', he said, looking up at me. 'I'm pretty sure they'll make for St Valéry now in the hope of being able to embark from there. Poor old 51st. You'll be worrying about your brother.' He touched my arm in sympathy. 'The French 10th Army has dithered until it is too late to put the Le Havre plan into practice.' He then hurried away with the information I had given him, leaving me very depressed about Colin.

Our midday meal, produced with some pride by three of Hallows' fitters, was a stew of tinned meat and vegetables heated in the vast, two-handled cooking pot from Hawkinge; we helped ourselves to ladlefuls of it. It was tasty enough, but for once I had no appetite and had to force myself to eat it, eyed anxiously by the cooks. Hallows reported three minor brushes with refugees wanting food and petrol.

I returned also undamaged from my next sortie, which I took care to be in the 51st area. I was able to confirm that Jameson had guessed correctly about St Valéry. The 51st together with the remnants of the French IXth Corps had formed a defensive perimeter around the port. Although I was lucky enough to have avoided enemy action, Chancery collected a number of bullet holes from ground machine-gun fire, and Holmes had been chased by two ME 109s. In evading them he had had to engage his over-ride power for much longer than the specified permissible time, and we were worried about the effect on his engines. Apart from take-off, it was our practice not to use more than three-quarters of the available power in order to cut down wear and tear.

As had happened to Jameson at Coulommiers, Robinson's evening visit coincided with our ablutions in our stream, much to his pleased amusement. We invited him to join us, which he did as quickly as he could strip, greatly enjoying the bathe and the use of my rapidly shrinking cake of soap.

Before he left, we went into the hangar for him to tell Sergeant Hallows his efforts in difficult circumstances were known and appreciated. As we were coming out, he stopped me and pointed smiling towards an open side-door into the hangar; there, standing against the wall, was an orderly row of four entrenching tools standing upright on their mattock blades with rolls of lavatory paper threaded onto their handles; and, as we were looking, one of the young airmen with a shy smile at us, came through the door and added another roll-loaded entrenching tool to the line.

'There you are!' Robinson smiled at me. 'The results of your talk this morning. How pleasing for you!'

'Yes,' said Hallows. 'Thank you, sir. That was just the job, and a great help to me.'

I suppose I should have felt pleased, but the battle news made our domestic arrangements, however important health-wise, seem very trivial. I longed to do something to help the 51st and Colin.

CHAPTER 7

CHARTRES –
THE CATHEDRAL

The following day, 11 June, a despatch rider from Robinson brought a message at midday instructing me to be on the steps leading to the main entrance of Chartres Cathedral at 21.30 hrs that evening, to meet Jameson, who would be passing there with the two French intelligence officers. In an added scribbled note, Jameson apologised for asking me to find my way to the cathedral, but, because of the crowded conditions of the roads, he and his party could not afford the time to divert off their route to our airfield. He had chosen the cathedral as an easily identified rendezvous point.

That afternoon Holmes was again chased and only escaped by flying at full power very low round obstacles. On the way home his cylinder-head temperatures were reading dangerously high, and an oil change revealed ominous flecks of metal in the sump.

Under normal conditions his aircraft would not have been fit to fly, but for him and his crew the alternative to risking flying the Blenheim back to England was to join the retreat by road to Nantes of the remaining units of our strike group. They had no doubt as to what they wanted to do, and, after Hallows and his men had completed what relatively little they could do, Holmes took off that evening and headed for Cherbourg and Warmwell. He only made the crossing with luck and landed at Andover on one engine. We missed him and his unfailing good humour.

Our unit was now reduced to nineteen and two Blenheims. We were all fit and well, but could only hope for the best about the aircraft, putting our faith in their robustness.

As a result of their frequent meetings over the last two weeks, Chancery and Jameson had become good friends, and it was obvious to me that Chancery wanted to come with me to meet him. Accordingly, when the time came, Hallows dropped us in the 3-tonner near the cathedral. Although I was not keen to lose more sleep than necessary, and did not relish walking the 3 miles back to our little airfield after meeting Jameson, I sent Hallows back in the 3-tonner; I was worried about it being hi-jacked if we kept it idle in Chartres, which was in a distressing state. The streets were filthy and crowded with refugees; the water and electricity supplies only worked spasmodically; there were queues at all the food shops of customers hoping they would open in spite of the late hour; but the saddest feature was the overall air of resignation. More than ever was I struck by the contrast with the cheerful, purposeful atmosphere at our little encampment in its corner of the airfield.

The pavements around the cathedral were crowded with refugees, as were the steps leading up to the main entrance. The people, lying or sitting with their belongings, were eyeing us in our flying overalls and forage caps, if not in an openly hostile manner, certainly in a way which showed they were not prepared to help us. It was only with difficulty that we found space on the steps to sit down and wait for Jameson.

When an hour went by without him, we were both feeling ready for a drink. I had noticed a bistro opposite which, unusually, was open, but surprisingly did not seem to be busy. We decided to investigate and immediately found out why it was not being patronised much. According to a notice pinned to the door, W. Grammond, the proprietor, was charging an entrance fee of 100 francs. We were not short of money as we had had little opportunity to spend any. Without hesitating, we opened the door, cash in hand, and went in to be met by a gigantic hairy man, whom we rightly presumed to be Monsieur Grammond, seated at a table. We were very pleasantly surprised by our reception, because we had become used to being made to feel not wanted. He jumped to his feet waving aside our proffered francs, crying, '*Vive l'Angleterre! Vive le Royale Air Force! Entrez! Entrez!*' The other customers smiled their welcome and moved to make seats empty for us. We were soon enjoying large strong cups of coffee and cognac, and delicious they were. We sat very contentedly at our table from where we could watch the cathedral steps, sipping and listening to the conversation of Monsieur Grammond's local, clearly tax-exempt, friends.

It was soon evident to us that, in the general opinion, it was only a matter of time before military resistance to the Germans ceased entirely in France, the possibility of holding out in a redoubt such as the Brittany peninsula being discounted.

The majority thought that their government would depart overseas as the Dutch, Belgians and Norwegians had done, and continue the fight from there. Some thought that 'overseas' would be in the considerable French colonies in North Africa; others opted for London. There was a general bitterness about their politicians' reliance on the Maginot Line, and about our military contribution being far too small. The latter, something which we had never considered, came as a shock to Chancery and me. I suppose we had been blinded by our own personal involvement, but we were made to realise how very few soldiers we had put into the field in comparison with them, the French.

We were nonplussed by being asked if we thought our government would seek peace terms from Hitler when we were on our own. Our obvious astonishment at such an idea caused general laughter, but, when we were asked penetrating questions about how we thought we would beat the Germans, even if we succeeded in preventing them from over-running us, we found ourselves giving vague, broad-brush answers. In truth, we had no idea.

One of our new friends obviously thought things were becoming far too serious, because he started playing 'J'attendrai' softly on his mouth-organ. Very soon, Monsieur Grammond went over to him and whispered something in his ear. He broke off his very popular sentimental lament, and started playing the tune of 'Colonel Bogey' to loud laughter and applause. Then, with Monsieur Grammond conducting his customers, they started roaring out a song in English with heavily French-accented words. I was hearing it for the first time, and afterwards I often thought of it as an anthem of the French resistance movement.

'Itler 'as only got one ball.

Goering 'as two but very small.

'Immler is somewhat *similaire*.

But poor old Goebbels 'as no balls at all!

We had grown so used, in the gloom of the retreat, to being depressed by the defeatist atmosphere all round our little unit that this robust, defiant attitude of Monsieur Grammond and his friends was a huge surprise, and gave us an immense boost. We found ourselves joining in the loud laughter, crying '*Bravo!*

Bravo! nos amis!' and going round the group shaking hands, slapping shoulders, and touching wine glasses as we drank toasts to each other.

Eventually, Monsieur Grammond said apologetically that he ought to close before the gendarmes intervened. We were amazed to find we had spent three hours there. With kind concern Monsieur Grammond offered us somewhere to sleep, but we explained about our tryst with Jameson. Monsieur Grammond and his friends came to the door of the bistro to bid us a noisy farewell, and we parted with much goodwill.

As Chancery wanted to look inside the cathedral, I kept watch outside on the steps, moving about as much as I could in the press of people to keep warm in the pre-dawn chill, and wondering what had happened to Jameson, now four hours late.

When Chancery rejoined me after some twenty minutes, he was obviously deeply moved. 'Alastair,' he said softly, yet firmly, 'you must go inside. Amazing sight! Amazing atmosphere! I'd no idea! I'm not much of a God botherer, but please go and see for yourself.'

Without a word, wondering what had so affected him, I left him on the steps and went through the

ALASTAIR PANTON & VICTORIA PANTON BACON

main entrance to face a truly amazing spectacle. The vast, upper reaches of the interior of the cathedral were mainly in shadow, but at ground level thousands and thousands of candles were burning. They burned, as far as I could see, in an unbroken line all the way round from one side of the entrance to the other. At the altars of the various side chapels the line of candles swelled into thick masses of flame with a particularly massive concentration in front of the main altar. Every pew and chair and almost every available piece of floor space was occupied by worshippers and refugees; kneeling, lying, sitting and standing; praying, talking, eating, drinking and sleeping. The air was murmurous with soft words. Acolytes moved about with difficulty, swinging censers. I stood gazing in wonder; the force of the massed prayer seemed an almost measurable factor; and, agnostic as I was, I felt growing in me a hope of eventual peace and of right prevailing in the end.

When I rejoined Chancery outside on the steps, something happened which set the seal on a totally unexpected, lastingly memorable experience. Through a small break in the heavily overcast sky, a brilliant beam from the newly risen sun struck the cathedral tower, isolating it from the surrounding shadows.

As we stood transfixed, I heard a soft chuckle at my side. A monk was smiling at us and waving gently at the illuminated tower. 'The German soldiers have "Gott mit uns" on their belt buckles. Who is right?' he asked quietly, and added, 'God bless you, my sons' as he moved away. The monk's gentle cynicism brought us back to the loaded present.

Shortly afterwards a car stopped on the roadway, and we saw Jameson waving to us. We hurried over to join him and the two French officers with him. We stood in the road in a tight group on the off-side of the car, talking in low voices so that we could not be overheard. 'What about the 51st?' I asked urgently. 'Did they get away all right?'

Before he answered I knew with a sickening feeling, by looking at him and the two Frenchmen, that something disastrous had happened. 'It's cursed bad luck,' he said. 'We've just heard that fog came down at night-fall to stop any question of evacuation. We're waiting now to hear what's happening. But it can't be good for the 51st. What have you to report?'

'I wish we had some good news for you,' I replied, 'but I'm afraid we haven't.' I turned to the map, which Chancery had flattened on the bonnet of Jameson's car, pointing. 'The Germans have crossed the Seine in several places, here, here and here.' The French officers were particularly interested in the points Chancery had marked on the map. We spoke in English and occasionally we had to pause while Jameson cleared a point in French for the benefit of his two colleagues. Once Chancery and I together interrupted him in French to correct something he said to the other two, which made them laugh. Under the dismal circumstances, and for the place and time of day, it was a particularly friendly, cheerful meeting.

The French officers asked us some more questions which we answered as best we could, and they told us that the French government had moved from Paris to Tours. Jameson then said he would not be seeing us again as he was being transferred to the staff of the British Commander-in-Chief, and Robinson would be dealing with us alone from then onwards. The French officers bade us a most courteous farewell. We parted from Jameson, exchanging words of genuine affection; he had been an understanding and good-humoured friend to us.

We set off a little wearily to walk the 3 miles back to the airfield, but after about fifteen minutes we were delighted and relieved to see the 3-tonner coming to meet us. Sergeant Hallows had been woken by guards changing over, had found out we had not returned, and had set out to see if he could help. As usual he had done the right thing without being told. He was a great hand and we both told him so. It was five o'clock before we sleeping-bagged ourselves, Hallows having been told we would not be taking off until midday. My last thought before I fell asleep was of the thousands of candles burning in the cathedral, miserably fearing that they boded ill for Colin and the 51st.

When we were woken five hours later by Robinson coming to brief us for the day's tasks, he began, 'Alastair, I am desperately sorry to tell you that the 51st came under direct fire from the cliffs to the east and west of their position. The French IXth Corps capitulated at eight o'clock, and what was left of the 51st surrendered at 10.30. I'm so sorry to give you such bad news.'

At first, I found it difficult to absorb the details of our tasks, hoping against hope that Colin was included in 'what was left of the 51st'. It was a relief when I succeeded in concentrating on the job in hand.

CHAPTER 8

LA FLÈCHE

From the tasks which Robinson gave us for the next two days, 12–13 June, it was clear that our interest now lay on the west end of the battle front. For three sorties in succession in the area at the base of the Normandy peninsula I saw no German troops at all, and this negative information gave obvious satisfaction. Meanwhile, Chancery was reporting movements across the west end of the Seine. It seemed to him that German armoured units would soon be in Paris, and they did, in fact, enter it the next day on 14 June. On that same day, it was no surprise to us to be on the move again, this time to La Flèche, near where our Headquarters had arrived on the Loir.

Once more, when I landed at La Flèche, soon to be followed by Chancery at the completion of our day's sorties, we found we were there before Hallows and the ground crew, and were having to refuel the aircraft ourselves. We found to our misgivings that both the usual small hangar and the refuelling point were within 20 yards of a country road crowded with refugees going south; but that we had to accept, there being no alternative landing space.

Once the refuelling was completed, I sent Farrow and Stride with Chancery's crew to see what domestic arrangements, if any, they could make. When they had gone, I sat with my back against the tyre of one of the aircraft wheels and continued with the Hugh Walpole I was reading. Chancery, who could sleep anywhere at any time, stretched out on the grass with his head on his parachute pack and went to sleep. That was how Hallows found us, and very glad I was to see him.

Farrow returned on his own with good news; not only had he found a well-sheltered stream nearby for our ablutions, but also a surprisingly helpful and friendly farmer, Groton by name, who had offered to let us use a large outhouse which had an arrangement for cooking his chicken and pig food. Stride and the other two aircrew sergeants were getting a fire going. By the time the miraculous ration lorry arrived, the 3-tonner had been unloaded into the hangar, and Hallows was able to send two airmen in it, together with the newly delivered rations, to help cook supper.

When a hungry and thirsty Robinson arrived, he was grateful to share our abundant supper in the outhouse. 'How well you have everything organised,' he said, between forkfuls of stew. 'If I didn't keep quiet about you, all sorts of people would be making excuses to visit you in the evenings.'

'I can't take any credit for the food,' I replied. 'I'm very lucky to have Stride doing all the arranging for what he calls our "crud".'

'Crud!' Robinson exclaimed. 'What a splendid word! I haven't heard that one before.'

'Oh! yes, sir,' Kingston joined in laughing. 'It's the "in" word nowadays, and you don't "eat" now, so much as "take crud aboard"!'

While we left Hallows and the well-fed airmen to clear away and wash up, Robinson and I went back to the hangar with Chancery and the five sergeants. 'I can confirm that the Germans have entered Paris,' he said. 'And they are moving almost unopposed at the moment south and east of Paris, but their advance is much more cautious west of Paris where we are

involved, and that's where you're needed tomorrow.'
He then went into our next day's flying tasks in detail,
before turning to speak directly to Hallows.

'I cannot stress too much, Sergeant Hallows, how
important these reconnaissances are, how important,
therefore, it is for you to keep the aircraft serviceable.
What's the position about the serviceability state?'

'Well, sir, we have to keep our fingers crossed,'
Hallows replied. 'We have only basic equipment, and
no power or facilities for using more equipment, if we
had it. The more we can keep revs and boost low the
better.' I felt particularly pleased about his instinctive
and unself-conscious use of 'we'; only Chancery and
I had control over the power settings in flight, but
Hallows spoke as if he were in the cockpit with us,
identifying himself completely with us.

The point was not lost on Robinson. As he was
leaving, he said to Hallows, 'You and your men are
doing a great job, and please tell them I said so.' As
he was mounting his motor-cycle, he said, 'Alastair,
my visits to you are a tonic. I wish I was with you all
the time.'

The next day's flying was memorable for one
untoward, unmilitary event. Hallows had put up a

small rectangular tent, some 8 feet by 4 feet, for the aircrew to use as a locker room and map store. About the only possession of mine there was a fleecy-lined Irvin flying jacket which Chancery's navigator had been using as a basis for his bed. In mid-afternoon. Chancery and I were away on our afternoon sorties; Hallows was in the hangar watching one of the fitters cleaning the plugs of the battery-charging motor; two of his party were at the farm cleaning out the fire and chopping sticks; four others he had sent to wash and do laundry in Farrow's stream; and the last two, the armed guards, were standing chatting at the further end of the hangar from our tent. Suddenly, one of the refugee cars turned off the road and raced across the few yards to the tent, brakes screeching to a halt. A woman and a younger man dragged a moaning, crying girl out of the car and hustled her into the tent, the flaps closing behind them.

One of the two guards, who had run across shouting in alarm, thrust his head into the tent and stood frozen in shock. As Hallows, alerted by the cries, came running, the poor young guard withdrew from the tent, and, paper-white, gasped, 'Sergeant, Sergeant, she's having a baby on Mr Panton's Irvin jacket!'

Although Hallows freely admitted afterwards that he was 'fair flummoxed' at first, he went quickly into action.

Although, as he said, he was a complete rookie as a midwife, he did know that hot water was needed in quantities. He immediately sent the pallid guard off to the farm in the 3-tonner to bring back as much as was quickly available. Fortunately he could speak a few words of French, and, when he told Madame Groton, the farmer's wife, why the water was needed, she quickly produced two huge steaming kettles, and came back in the 3-tonner rolling up her sleeves.

When I landed an hour and a half later, I could not understand why men were standing around grinning up at me in the cockpit. When I switched off, everyone tried at the same time to tell me what had happened. The importunate birth had been entirely successful; the baby and its mother were safely in the Grotons' farm with its father and grandmother; the tent had returned to normal except for the smell of carbolic; my Irvin jacket had been burned; and the poor boy who had made the discovery was already nicknamed 'Doc', because his diagnosis of the girl's complaint had been so quick and accurate!

The fine weather went on and on. In comparison

with the Dunkirk evacuation, my sorties had been remarkably and unexpectedly uneventful. As a result, when Farrow, Stride and I set off on our sortie early in the morning of 16 June, we felt we were carrying out what was merely a matter of routine.

We were very wrong.

At his briefing the evening before, Robinson had pointed out the temporary position of Headquarters, and said he needed to know the nearest German positions to it; near Chartres, he thought.

This estimate was based on what we had reported ourselves the day before. We started out casually, thinking we would not have to bother much for half an hour or so. I was looking round, thinking philosophical thoughts about the contrast between the loveliness of nature in a countryside smiling under the summer sun and the bestial havoc caused by nations at war. Then I heard in my earphones a gasp of consternation from Farrow. 'God Almighty, look at that!'

To see where he was pointing, I dipped my port wing and went into a steep turn to see a startling sight. On a road below us was a bridge with the middle section destroyed. Halted at the bridge, alongside the head of a long line of refugee cars, were four German tanks, some 120 miles nearer to our Headquarters than our intelligence estimation. I flew slowly round at a safe distance from machine-gun fire from the tanks, working things out. Clearly something had to be done immediately. I did not think the damaged bridge would hold the tanks up for long; the river it spanned was a small one, shallow after the long fine spell; and the tanks would soon find somewhere to cross.

Indeed, as I watched, two left the road to rumble along the river bank in one direction, and two in the other. If I went back to La Flèche, I would be little nearer our Headquarters than the German tanks, and I would only have the 3-tonner to carry the news to Headquarters along the crowded roads. I was not in radio contact with any ground station. I did not even have the wherewithal to adopt the old First World War tactic of dropping a message in a weighted bag. The only possibility was that I should find a field near the Headquarters where I could land and sound the alarm myself.

Within minutes of arriving at this conclusion, I was circling over the chateau which housed the

Headquarters, looking at the upturned faces of drivers of vehicles standing around it, not feeling very hopeful about landing safely nearby. I tried not to admit to myself that, if the worst came to the worst, my duty was to crash-land my Blenheim to save the Headquarters.

Then on my second circuit, I saw a Tiger Moth and a Lysander standing in the corner of a field, tucked in under some trees. Under normal circumstances, both these light aircraft required much shorter landing and take-off runs than my Blenheim, but circumstances were abnormal. It was that field or nothing, and I had to chance it. Fortunately, what little wind there was blew down the length of the field. I came in low and slow just above the stall; I felt my wheels brush through the top of a hedge; I gave a burst of power as the ground was coming up at me; I landed with less of a bump than I feared, but one which nevertheless made me wince; and I ran about 200 yards, stopping less than 50 feet from the hedge in front of me.

'Well done, sir! Bloody good!' I heard Farrow's voice in my earphones and saw him grinning round at me, while Stride's Canadian drawl added 'Piece of cake!' I turned the Blenheim round, feeling gratitude and apologies for the rough treatment of her flowing through my hands and feet onto the controls. I taxied back as near as possible to the hedge through which I had landed, lined up for take-off, and switched off.

'Don't leave the aircraft whatever you do,' I said to Farrow and Stride. 'I'm off to Headquarters.' I released my seat-straps and parachute harness, hung my helmet on the control column, grabbed my forage hat, and jumped out through the hatch. As I ran towards the chateau, I passed the pilots of the two aircraft and some ground crew approaching with looks of startled inquiry, calling out, 'Sorry I can't stop. See my crew.'

I ran across a lawn with flower-beds in it, crossed a gravelled area where cars stood, and rushed through large double doors which stood open. Inside them was a desk with two RAF policemen. 'Quick!' I gasped. 'Where's the Ops Room?'

'Identity card, please sir,' one said imperturbably. I longed to shout 'Oh! Balls!' at him, but instead I slid my identity card out of my breast pocket, and had an inspired thought that I needed their help.

'It's desperately urgent. I've seen German tanks not far away. One of you please take me to the Ops Room.'

The policeman who had asked to see my identity card remained splendidly unmoved as he entered the details of my card in his log, but his companion jumped to his feet saying, 'Follow me, sir!' He set off along a corridor as if excited, dishevelled, panting pilots were frequent visitors. I was grateful for his presence because I was conscious, as I passed, of being eyed curiously and none too kindly and I might well have been held up without his protective escort. We hurried up a shallow flight of steps into a small hall-way with a notice 'Operations Room' beside a door on which hung a detachable sign 'Do not disturb'.

Leaning against the wall and chatting were two smartly uniformed squadron leaders who eyed me in my crumpled flying overalls with disdain. 'What do you want?' asked one, emphasising 'you', lips looking as if they were about to curl.

'The C-in-C,' I replied, feeling protocol floating away down the steps.

'Oh! You do, do you?' was the reply. 'He's far too busy to see you.'

I felt a surge of elation as the chance for the crack of a lifetime was suddenly presented to me. 'Not as busy as he's going to be in a moment,' I snapped, and pushed past him, his colleague and their scandalised expressions, bursting open the door. I just had time to notice that only a crinkling round his eyes registered my policeman's amusement. As I stood in the doorway, I was aware of heads turning towards me from a group of senior officers seated round the C-in-C. They were grouped in front of a small, powerfully lighted dais on which Robinson, pointer in hand, was standing in front of a be-flagged map.

'Sir!' I cried, aiming at Robinson. 'I had to burst in. There are four German tanks only 30 miles away.'

With gasps of distress people were leaping to their feet, but I noticed with admiration the calmness of the C-in-C. He smiled in my direction as he picked up his hat.

'Thank you, my boy. It's just as well to know.' He turned to the now grinning Robinson. 'But who is this?'

'It's our Blenheim reconnaissance flight commander, Flight Lieutenant Panton.'

'Ah! Yes indeed! I should have guessed.' The air marshal patted me on the shoulder. 'Well done! Keep up the good work!' Then he turned to the rest of the gathering. 'Well, gentlemen. Tomorrow's move is brought forward to now.'

As the room emptied, I explained in detail to Robinson what had happened. He immediately agreed with what I had done, told me to continue with my interrupted sortie, and arranged to meet me at La Flèche that evening. 'But have a good look round before you land in case the Germans are there before me. Go to Nantes if they are.' He left chuckling. He did not say so to me, but I think he was highly amused at the uproar I had caused among some of the more staid and senior members of the Headquarters.

When I rejoined Farrow and Stride, I was grateful to see that the wind strength had increased and maintained its helpful direction for my take-off. It was as well that the wind had freshened because I only just cleared the far hedge, although I applied all the tricks for a short take-off which I knew.

Although we searched carefully along the river in both directions from the blown bridge, there was no sign of the German tanks having crossed the river. We never did find out what had happened to them, or what they were doing so far in front of the rest of the Germans. We, Robinson and ourselves, assumed that the four tanks had been sent to probe ahead of the main body, and, having been detected, had holed up until they could rejoin the main body of the German armour. This we found, more or less as expected, a mile or two south-west of Chartres.

After all the excitement of the morning, we were grateful that the rest of our sortie on our way back to La Flèche was uneventful. There, however, more shocks were in store for us. As I flew two slow circuits of the airfield before landing, I was dismayed to see that it was empty; Hallows and his party, the 3-tonner ,and all our equipment and kit had gone. I grumbled over the intercom to Farrow and Stride that, whatever was not clear to us, we would be refuelling ourselves again. As I taxied slowly towards the hangar with the now customary flattening of the long grass by our airscrews, I saw Monsieur Groton bicycling towards us from his farm, balancing the pump for the petrol tank on his handlebars. When I switched off and jumped out, he was smiling ruefully and muttering '*Quelle débâcle! Quelle débâcle!*' He handed me a piece of paper, a note from Hallows.

Flt. Lt. Panton, sir. We had just seen Mr Chancery off on his second sortie (I didn't like the sound of his port engine) when a Movements Officer from

Army Headquarters arrived, sounding very excited. He wanted to know what the hell we were doing here. Hadn't we heard that the Frogs had asked for an armistice without telling us? Hadn't we been told to get to St Nazaire by today? Anyhow, although I tried to argue, we had to pack up and go 'toute suite'. I've left a few bits and pieces for you with M. Groton. I have told him to give you or Mr Chancery this chit, whoever lands first. I hope you are OK, sir. I did not like leaving, nor did the rest of the lads, before we knew why you were late back this morning. See you in Blighty. Good Luck to you, sir, Farrow and Stride.

A. Hallows, Sergeant

I handed the note to Farrow and Stride who read it together and reacted predictably. Stride immediately said, 'We're up shit creek without a paddle now.' Farrow merely shrugged and smiled faintly. For myself I was deeply concerned that Hallows and his party had been separated from me so that I could not look after them, and deeply moved by his concern for us. I folded up his note and pocketed it, where I eventually found it together with the card containing the hygienic points I made in my address at the little airfield at Chartres.

I swallowed the lump in my throat and turned to Stride. 'We're not without a paddle yet,' I said, patting our Blenheim's wing. 'Not while she continues to be flyable. Come on. Let's get her refuelled.' This we proceeded to do, and were much touched when Monsieur Groton said he would like to help us and would fetch his son along as well. He cycled back to the farm, and, when he returned with his sixteen-year-old boy, Farrow and I handed over the pumping to them, leaving Stride to manage the nozzle and strainer at the various filling points on the aircraft. With Farrow, I went round topping up with engine oil, hydraulic fluid, distilled battery water, and air for the tyres.

When we had finished, the Grotons went back to their farm, accompanied by Farrow and Stride, who went to prepare supper. The rations had arrived just before Hallows left. I continued with Hugh Walpole, and had half an hour's peace. Then Chancery arrived, flying a circuit before landing. I observed his short flight carefully, and was relieved to see his engines seemed to be running reasonably well. As soon as he throttled back to land, however, the pops, bangs and black smoke which came from his port engine justified Hallows' misgivings. When Chancery switched off, he leaned out of his cockpit window, smiling ruefully and shaking his head. 'I was chased by 109s again,' he said, 'and being on full power has just about done for my port engine. It's not too bad at cruising revs, but the slow running is terrible. I only hope it will start again.' He paused, and his expression changed as he looked round. 'By the way, where are all the others?'

'They've gone to be evacuated,' I said. 'We're on our own.'

'Oh, my God!' he exclaimed and then looked resigned. 'But I don't expect it makes much difference. Hallows could not have changed the engine, which is what I expect is needed, but I would have liked a plug change.'

When he had climbed out and joined me, I said,

As soon as I heard your port engine when you throttled back, clattering and banging away and pushing out all that black smoke, I knew you would have to go back home, if you could. It's no good staying here in that condition, even if we had any ground crew.

'Yes, I suppose so,' he agreed gloomily. 'I've so enjoyed being out here, especially the last ten days with you. I had hoped to see the show through to the end, but there it is.'

'Well then,' I said, 'if you think you can make it, you had better go this evening after we've refuelled you, and you've had a meal. Things seem pretty quiet and I doubt if German fighters are about now. God knows what will happen tomorrow.'

He agreed unwillingly, and we had started to tackle the refuelling of his Blenheim when we were completely taken aback by Madame Groton appearing with the husband of the girl who had given birth on my Irvin jacket, saying that, as her husband and son were busy with the cattle, they had come to take their place with the refuelling. Chancery and I could only stammer our thanks and admire Madame Groton's sturdy strength on the pump handle.

Meanwhile Farrow and Stride, mainly Stride, had been working wonders with the plentiful rations in our outhouse. Not only had they produced a three-course meal of vegetable soup creamed with dried milk, corned beef hash in his best dry Canadian style with mashed potatoes and green peas, and creamed rice with peaches, all out of tins except for the Grotons' potatoes, but they had made enough to invite the four Grotons and the new parents and grandmother to join us. Hallows had left wine and beer in some abundance for us, for which Farrow had borrowed glasses from the farmhouse. After the refuelling of Chancery's Blenheim was completed, thirteen of us had a splendid meal with the new-born baby warding off bad luck by being present in a basket. The four sergeants, helped by Groton junior and the new father, took it in turns to guard the two Blenheims. In the dark days to come, I often thought of that happy meal and our helpful, friendly, brave guests.

Shortly after eight o'clock that evening we all went down to the airfield to see Chancery and his crew off. After a few anxious moments his port engine fired with a great gout of black smoke, and then ran smoothly, if a little fast. We all stood watching him take off, circle round, and give us the farewell salute of a shallow dive. He disappeared in a north-westerly direction towards Cherbourg and Warmwell. I was optimistic that all would be well; it was a calm, clear evening; there was little risk of being troubled by German activity at that time of day and in that part of the country; and his oiling, ailing port engine had to keep going only for another hour and a half or so.

When all the Groton party had left to go back to the farm, after insisting that I should see them before I left, Farrow and Stride accompanied them to clear up the remains of the feast and pack some rations for us to take away with us. I sat back against a Blenheim main wheel, with my Hugh Walpole and my 0.38 revolver beside me, to await Robinson.

I could not avoid a forlorn and lonely feeling, intensified by the continuing unbroken stream of uncaring refugees. The two aircraft, two pilots, four aircrew and ten ground crew of that morning had been reduced to our Blenheim, Farrow, Stride and myself. I needed Robinson's cheery morale-restoring arrival half-an-hour later and his cry of 'Ah! The last of the Mohicans, I see. Chancery not back yet? I hope he's all right.'

'Well, only just,' I said.

He was chased by a 109 this morning and that did his port engine no good at all. We decided that he really needed an engine change, and it was no good keeping him here. I sent him back home, and he left a short time ago. I hope you agree.

'Yes, of course. If Hallows could not do what was needed, there was no alternative.' He paused and looked round. 'Where are Hallows and all his chaps, by the way?'

'When I was away on my second sortie this morning, a movements officer turned up and raised a rumpus with Hallows because he was still here, and ordered him to go to St Nazaire.' I handed Robinson the note Hallows left me, which he read with a deepening frown.

'There's been a stupid cock-up somewhere. I had arranged for Hallows and his chaps to be flown out when you had finished here. However,' he shrugged philosophically, 'things are moving pretty swiftly now. We'll have to do our best without them.' He was not to know the tragic consequences of our being parted from our ground crew, as he continued.

We've only a day or two left. The Canadians, who have only just disembarked at Cherbourg, are re-embarking there. I believe our Prime Minister is trying to persuade the French government, which is now at Bordeaux, to withdraw to North Africa and fight on from there. What I need you to do for me is to keep an eye on the Germans who may be trying to cut off our retreat to Cherbourg and the Brittany ports. But can you do it on your own without any ground crew?

'If the aircraft keeps serviceable, sir,' I replied, 'I can easily cover the area myself for two days, provided, of course, I don't get shot down.'

'Yes,' he said in an absent-minded tone, 'you have a point there.' Suddenly his expression changed. 'By Jove!' he cried delightedly. 'You shook the Headquarters this morning. They fairly hurtled off in a panic. Look what I found in the Accounts Section!' He opened an attache case and showed me thousands and thousands of new 100-franc notes in bundles.

I believe some of our chaps haven't been paid for some time. Perhaps I can equalise things a bit if I can catch up with them. I'd love to give it away before I have to hand it in. However, let's get down to business, your business. What have you to report?

I told him the result of my one sortie and Chancery's two, which were much as expected. When he had marked the positions on his map and taken some notes, he said, 'Now for tomorrow. You'll be all right here for tonight, won't you?'

'Yes,' I replied, 'as far as the Germans are concerned, but, without any guards, we shall have to sleep in the Blenheim. Otherwise it will be stripped and milked of fuel by refugees, or spivs, or both.'

'As bad as that, is it?'

'Yes it is.'

'Well, keep going. It won't be for much longer I'm afraid. Land from your first sortie at Vertun, just south of Nantes here.' He pointed to his map. 'If I can't be there myself, I'll send someone else to see you. But I'll certainly be there in the evening.'

The next day, 17 June, Farrow, Stride and I went early to have a farewell cup of coffee with the Grotons in their kitchen. Just before we left Monsieur Groton surprised me by taking me aside, gripping my arm and whispering with concerned emphasis, 'My dear friend, take my advice, be very careful whom you trust.' Then we shook hands all round and wished each other luck with remarks about '*après la guerre*,' tried to ignore the ladies' tears, and took off without saying much to each other.

We carried out a thorough search of the approaches to Cherbourg, in which we saw heavy fighting. We had just passed Carentan going southwards when, of all things, we had a 'victory' over a German aircraft. I was flying slowly and very low, at about 30 feet, along the side of a wood at which Farrow and Stride were peering through binoculars. I turned sharply to follow the line of trees. As I did so, I found myself meeting head-on a light high-wing monoplane. I just had time to pull back on my control column. The aircraft passed beneath me so close that I could not believe we had avoided a collision, so close that I could see the two occupants of the cockpit gape at me in horror and throw up their arms as if to protect their faces. I put on full power and went into a vertical turn to see the aircraft, which I now recognised to be a Fiesler Storch, hit the ground heavily and bounce twice, shedding pieces before coming to a droop-winged stop. The two Germans erupted from the cockpit and pelted away to stop and shake their fists at us in fury as we circled. We continued on our way, chuckling at our unarmed victory over them, who had been so unlucky as to meet head-on, and very low down, the only British aircraft within perhaps 200 miles or so.

On our way to Vertun we passed over the large airfield at Nantes which, littered with abandoned equipment, showed every sign of the end of a retreat. We had been looking forward to retailing our comic downing of the Storch, but, about half an hour after we had landed, and while we were refuelling, an RAF intelligence officer, sent by Robinson for our reconnaissance report, appeared with news which put a stop to any light-heartedness. That morning, at the port of St Nazaire some 40 miles away, the troopship *Lancastria*, crammed with RAF troops, had been bombed and sunk with a large loss of life. We, of course, immediately thought of Hallows and his party, hoping that they had not been on board, but dreading they had.

When we saw Robinson that evening, he told us that late the evening before in Nantes he had gone into the Dome, a large restaurant with several bars. The Dome and the surrounding area was packed with tired, thirsty, penniless RAF troops awaiting embarkation, whom the locals would not serve without payment.

'Just as I imagined it would yesterday evening at La Flèche,' continued Robinson,

the money I nicked from the Headquarters came in very useful. I stood by one of the bars handing out 100 franc notes as the troops filed past. It caused a local inflation, because, as money became available, the local gentry put up prices. By the way, as I was leaving, Sergeant Hallows button-holed me. He had still some money left out of your imprest for himself and his lot and didn't need any cash, but he was very anxious for news of you. I told him about your landing at Headquarters making you late back, and about your supper party with the Grotons. He looked so pleased to hear you were safe.

'Do you think he was on the *Lancastria*?' I asked.

'I expect so. Why?' Robinson looked puzzled, and I then realised that he had not, by some quirk of circumstance, heard about the bombing. He was considerably shaken when I told him. 'Oh my God! Oh my God!' he muttered quietly to himself. Among the 3,000 RAF lives lost in that attack on the *Lancastria*, as we later found out, were Hallows and all his men. They had been killed simply as a result of staff confusion, which had prevented them being flown home.[1]

After a pause, while he collected his thoughts, Robinson said with a wry smile,

It's a case of John Masefield's novel 'Odtaa', One Damn Thing After Another. Here we are stuck in France, trying to do our best against the Germans with slender resources and with the minimum of help from the French. Their government at Bordeaux, now under Marshal Pétain, has asked the Germans for an armistice without even informing our ambassador. All official resistance from the French has finished. Where does that leave people like us?

I thought with considerable affection of Madame Foullens in Poix, the Montaignes at Coulommiers, Monsieur Grammond and his undaunted customers in the Chartres bistro, and the Grotons at La Flèche.

---

1 On 17 June 1940, more than 3,000 servicemen, civilian women and children were drowned during their journey home from France to England after their ship, the *Lancastria*, was bombed by German planes. They were among some 6,000 people on board the converted Cunard liner. The tragedy, which took place near the Brittany port of Saint-Nazaire, was the worst maritime disaster of the Second World War.

'I think we shall always find some people who will do what they can for us, but all the time the considerable risks they will be running will be increasing.'

I agree, Alastair, and it is up to us not to expose our friends to danger. What this amounts to is that in principle we have got to rely only on ourselves. Until recently, I thought that at the worst no French people would take active steps to prevent what is left of us extricating ourselves. Now I am not so sure. Two or three days ago in the south of France, civilians, fearful of German reprisals, had driven lorries across an airfield to stop our aircraft bombing Italy.

After a short pause to light one of the thin cigars Stride had given him, Robinson continued gloomily, 'I suppose it is logical to conclude that it is not beyond the bounds of possibility that we might be arrested by some French authority and handed over to the Germans by way of ingratiating themselves.'

As he voiced this hitherto unimaginable possibility, I suddenly remembered Monsieur Groton at La Flèche. 'You may well be right, sir. When we were saying goodbye to the Grotons at La Flèche, he did tell me not to trust anyone. At the time, in the emotional atmosphere, I did not fully appreciate the warning he was trying to give me.'

Stride with his usual enterprise produced mugs of hot coffee which we were gratefully enjoying when a Tiger Moth landed, taxied over to us, and switched off. When the pilot took off his goggles and helmet, I recognised the grinning face of Charles Ramsden, late of 13 Squadron at Odiham, and now a squadron leader. A fluent French speaker, he was an assistant air attaché on our ambassador's staff.

'Alastair!' he cried. 'What on earth are you doing here? Hasn't anybody told you to bugger off? Everyone else has scarpered, I'm sure. I'm on my way down to Bordeaux, if I can get some petrol for this little chap.' He patted the fuselage affectionately. 'I call it my "*Sauve qui peut*". For this last day or two I haven't dared take my eyes off it in case some sod pinched it to bunk back to England in it. Can you refuel me?'

Luckily Farrow had uncovered some tins of petrol suitable for the Tiger Moth, which needed a lower octane than our Blenheim. We soon had the refuelling done, and fed Ramsden some coffee and bully-beef sandwiches.

'I'm waiting for Squadron Leader Robinson,' I explained.

'I wouldn't wait too long,' he said, 'if I were in your shoes. The Germans are all over the place. I'm off to Bordeaux, thanks to your help. I'm going there because, if Paul Reynaud succeeds in his plan to take his government to North Africa, I'm going with it.'

'What about this armistice?' I asked.

'God knows,' he said cheerily. 'It's a real bugger's muddle.' It was. With a final word to me to look after myself 'because no one else can', he flew off to the south.

I tried to read my Walpole, but Ramsden's remarks had done nothing for my peace of mind. I envied the calmness of Farrow and Stride stretched out on the grass, happy to leave all the decisions to me. I wished I did not feel so jumpy, worrying among other things whether the engines would start when the time came. Eventually, half-way through the afternoon, some two hours late, Robinson arrived on a motorbike.

'Gosh! I'm so glad to see you,' I said, as he removed his helmet. 'With everyone advising me not to hang around, the last twelve hours have lasted a long time.'

'Yes,' he said. 'I'm sorry you've had to wait for me, and I'm very grateful. It's been grim for you, but we're finished here now, and I'm coming with you. We have to look at the fighting around Cherbourg, and then go across to Brest to report there. Then home!'

We wasted no time climbing into the Blenheim, Farrow sitting in Robinson's lap for the take-off, before going forward to his navigating table in the nose. The starboard engine started immediately. The port engine was very sluggish, and the batteries were beginning to labour by the time it fired. My mouth was very dry by then.

We saw the last transport ship leaving Cherbourg with the German armour closing on the harbour. When I was writing this story fifty years later, I learned with some interest from Churchill's *The Second World War* that the German commander was the famous General Rommel, who had also surrounded my brother Colin's 51st Division at St Valéry.

From Cherbourg we flew across to Brest. A car with an intelligence officer was waiting on the airfield, and, saying quite unnecessarily 'Don't switch off', because nothing would have persuaded me to do so, Robinson jumped out. He hurried to the car with his maps, reported what we had seen, and within five minutes or so was back strapped into his seat.

'Right ho!' His voice came cheerfully over the intercom. 'That's it. Done. Finished. Home, James, and don't spare the horses.'

Thankfully I took off and headed for Warmwell at a comfortable 1,500 feet over the shining sea. We saw nobody and presumably nobody saw us. Gradually, I felt a glow of relief spreading over me as we left poor, shattered France behind, with the Dorset coast lying ahead in the evening sun

This is the Blenheim Alastair flew on 14 July 1940, after it fell. By this point, Alastair would have been captured, and his prisoner of war years were just beginning.

Photograph kindly sourced and supplied by the Blenheim Society

Page from RAF Operations Record Book detailing Alastair Panton's flght on 14 July 1940 – note in the remarks section: 'Aircraft Failed to Return.'

Document supplied by the National Archives, Kew.

CHAPTER 9

END PIECE

At Warmwell, where Robinson left us with kind words for us all, I learned that 53 Squadron had been moved from Eastchurch to Gatwick. We flew on there and I landed at about nine o'clock as the sun was setting. I went up to the building which had been commandeered as our mess, carrying the suitcase I had packed at Eastchurch, and not opened. The first person I met in the hall was Holmes.

'Oh, boss!' He beamed. 'We've been wondering when you'd get back. Is Ray Chancery with you?'

I dropped my suitcase, gaping at him. 'Oh, no! Not him too! He should have been back two days ago.' He and his crew were never heard of again, and I can only assume that he disappeared into the Channel with engine failure.

Robinson was killed in 1942 on the Takoradi run, ferrying a Hurricane from Nigeria to Egypt where he had been posted to command a fighter wing. Holmes, now flying fighters, was killed in Burma in 1944. In that same year, one of his Blenheim crew was killed in a collision with another Lancaster over Hamburg. The other member of his crew, also in a Lancaster, was killed by night-fighters over Munich.

In July 1940 I was firing at a Messerschmitt 110 over Belgium, near Brussels. I saw smoke coming from it, and it exploded just before a fire took hold in my Blenheim, probably from some incendiary bullet I had collected. I managed to crash-land my plane but was taken prisoner on landing and moved to a burns hospital. Nearly five years later, when the war in Europe came to an end in May 1945, I was returned home.

Even by 18 June 1940, the purposeful, yet almost carefree atmosphere I met at Coulommiers on 7 June seemed a long time ago. It was difficult to believe that only eleven days had elapsed in which the humiliation of France was completed. Of the twenty-two members of our unit whom I met there, sixteen were already dead. Four more were killed or died later on in the war. The average number of bomber operations completed over Germany by aircrew was ten. Farrow completed sixty-five and, like Bence, became a school-master. Only Farrow, Bence and I survived the war.

Notice regarding Royal Air Force awards, approved by the king in March 1940, listing seven recipients of the Distinguished Flying Cross, including Alastair Panton.

Document kindly sourced and supplied by Andrew Cormack, Keeper of Fine Arts, Medals and Uniforms at RAF Hendon.

CENTRAL CHANCERY OF THE ORDERS OF KNIGHTHOOD

St. James's Palace, S.W.1.
2nd January, 1950.

The KING has been graciously pleased to give orders for the following appointments to the Most Excellent Order of the British Empire :—

To be an Ordinary Commander of the Military Division of the said Most Excellent Order :—

Brigadier (temporary) James Richard Glencoe ANGUS, D.S.O. (17888), late Infantry, Commandant, The Malay Regiment.

To be an Ordinary Officer of the Military Division of the said Most Excellent Order :—

Brigadier (local) Carol ARDERN (15616), Royal Regiment of Artillery, Officer Commanding Troops, Bermuda.

CENTRAL CHANCERY OF THE ORDERS OF KNIGHTHOOD

St. James's Palace, S.W.1.
2nd January, 1950.

The KING has been graciously pleased to give orders for the following promotions in, and appointments to, the Most Excellent Order of the British Empire :—

To be Ordinary Knights Commanders of the Military Division of the said Most Excellent Order :—

Air Vice-Marshal Alexander Paul DAVIDSON, C.B., C.B.E., Royal Air Force.
Air Vice-Marshal Anthony Lauderdale PAXTON, C.B., C.B.E., D.F.C., Royal Air Force.

To be Ordinary Commanders of the Military Division of the said Most Excellent Order :—

Acting Air Commodore John Maxwell, Royal Air Force.
Acting Air Commodore Herbert Martin MASSEY, M.C., Royal Air Force.
Acting Air Commodore John William MONCUR, M.I.C.E., Royal Air Force.
Acting Air Commodore Walter Philip George PRETTY, O.B.E., Royal Air Force.
Group Captain Bernard Leslie BLOFIELD, Royal Air Force.
Group Captain Edward Hugh Markham DAVIS, O.B.E., Royal Air Force.
Group Captain Andrew HARVEY, M.B. B.Ch., D.P.H., Royal Air Force.
Group Captain Richard Rupert NASH, Royal Air Force.
Acting Group Captain Frank Henry BEDFORD, O.B.E., M.C., M.M., Royal Air Force.
Group Captain Ronald Joseph COHEN, A.F.C., Royal New Zealand Air Force.

To be Ordinary Officers of the Military Division of the said Most Excellent Order :—

Group Officer Mary Henrietta BARNETT, Women's Royal Air Force.
Group Captain Joseph Cox, D.F.C., C.M.G., Royal Air Force.
Acting Group Captain Arnold WALL, Royal Air Force.

Wing Commander Otto Maxwell BERKELEY (73519), Royal Air Force.
Wing Commander Reginald Henry Clifford BURWELL, D.F.C. (40002), Royal Air Force.
Wing Commander Edward George CLARKE (35345), Royal Air Force.
Wing Commander George Augustus Erskine HARKNESS, A.F.C. (27657), Royal Air Force.
Wing Commander Frederick Charles HORNSBY-SMITH (74901), Royal Air Force.
Wing Commander Walter KERSWELL (44087), Royal Air Force.
Wing Commander James LAMBIE (21158), Royal Air Force.
Wing Commander Peter Alan McWHANNELL (34024), Royal Air Force.
Wing Commander Harold John MAGUIRE, D.S.O. (34048), Royal Air Force.
Wing Commander Alastair Dyson PANTON, D.F.C. (33331), Royal Air Force.
Wing Commander Thomas William PIPER, A.F.C. (37913), Royal Air Force.
Wing Commander Bryan SAMSON (34249), Royal Air Force.
Wing Commander Cyril Victor STAMMERS, M.B.E. (46085), Royal Air Force.
Wing Commander Léopold Herbert STEWART (13250), Royal Air Force.
Acting Wing Commander Alan HARTLEY (64049), Royal Air Force Volunteer Reserve.
Acting Wing Commander William John MARSHALL, M.B.E. (43454). Royal Air Force.
Acting Wing Commander John Belmont TAYLOR (72177), Royal Air Force.
Principal Matron Margaret Ellen GARNETT, R.R.C. (3019), Princess Mary's Royal Air Force Nursing Service (Retired).

To be Ordinary Members of the Military Division of the said Most Excellent Order :—

Squadron Leader Arthur Berlin TANK, A.F.C. (43173), Royal Air Force.
Squadron Leader Geoffrey Herbert THOMAS (46574), Royal Air Force.
Squadron Leader Alan Ridgard TOWERS (44296), Royal Air Force.
Squadron Leader Sidney William WALLER (31489), Royal Air Force.
Acting Squadron Officer Eileen Joyce BOBLASE (5795), Women's Royal Air Force.
Acting Squadron Leader Walter Morton COCKSON, M.I.Mon and Cy.E. (109176), Royal Air Force.
Acting Squadron Leader William James GREENSLADE (117768), Royal Air Force.
Acting Squadron Leader Hugh Philip HOWKINS, A.F.C. (44826), Royal Air Force.
Acting Squadron Leader Lionel Harley OATES (111682), Royal Air Force.
Acting Squadron Leader Cyril Thomas PHILLIPS, D.F.C. (143413), Royal Air Force.
Flight Lieutenant John GILLESPIE (160791), Royal Air Force.
Flight Lieutenant Harold Reginald GARRETT (51998), Royal Air Force.
Flight Lieutenant Henry Norman KITCHIN (43566), Royal Air Force.
Flight Lieutenant Kenneth Charles LOUMES (50702), Royal Air Force.
Flight Officer Edith May MACGREGOR (5882), Women's Royal Air Force.

K.C.B.

To be Ordinary Members of the Military Division of the Second Class, or Knights Commanders, of the said Most Honourable Order :—

Lieutenant-General Cecil Hugh BLACKER, C.B., O.B.E., M.C. (67083), late Royal Armoured Corps.

Lieutenant-General John Noel THOMAS, C.B., D.S.O., M.C. (66504), late Corps of Royal Engineers, Colonel Commandant Corps of Royal Engineers, Colonel Commandant Royal Pioneer Corps, Honorary Colonel Liverpool University O.T.C.

C.B.

To be Ordinary Members of the Military Division of the Third Class, or Companions, of the said Most Honourable Order :—

Major-General Edwin Frederick FOXTON, O.B.E. (72136), late Royal Army Educational Corps.
Major-General Allan McGILL, C.B.E. (384378), late Corps of Royal Electrical and Mechanical Engineers.
Major-General Robert Bernard PENFOLD, M.V.O. (375887), late Royal Regiment of Artillery.
Major-General Charles Herbert STAINFORTH, O.B.E. (378504), late Royal Army Service Corps.
Major-General Gerald Abson WHITFIELD, O.B.E. (143327), Army Legal Services.
Major-General Reginald WHITWORTH, C.B.E. (124159), late Foot Guards.

(MINISTRY OF DEFENCE (AIR FORCE DEPARTMENT))

K.C.B.

To be an Ordinary Member of the Military Division of the Second Class, or Knight Commander, of the said Most Honourable Order :—

Air Marshal Denis Graham SMALLWOOD, C.B., C.B.E., D.S.O., D.F.C., Royal Air Force.

C.B.

To be Ordinary Members of the Military Division of the Third Class, or Companions, of the said Most Honourable Order :—

Air Vice-Marshal Thomas James HANLON, C.B.E., Royal Air Force.
Air Vice-Marshal Michael Henry LE BAS, C.B.E., D.S.O., A.F.C., Royal Air Force.
Air Vice-Marshal John Hunter HUNTER-TOD, O.B.E., Royal Air Force.
Acting Air Vice-Marshal Stanley Hadian BONSER, M.B.E., Royal Air Force.
Air Commodore Alastair Dyson PANTON, O.B.E., D.F.C., Royal Air Force.

Order of the Bath
(Civil Division)

G.C.B.

To be an Ordinary Member of the Civil Division of the First Class, or Knight Grand Cross, of the said Most Honourable Order :—

Sir Ludovic James DUNNETT, K.C.B., C.M.G., Permanent Under-Secretary of State, Ministry of Defence.

K.C.B.

To be Ordinary Members of the Civil Division of the Second Class, or Knights Commanders, of the said Most Honourable Order :—

Cyril Maxwell Palmer BROWN, C.B., C.M.G., Second Permanent Secretary, Board of Trade.
Samuel GOLDMAN, C.B., Second Secretary, H.M. Treasury.

C.B.

To be Ordinary Members of the Civil Division of the Third Class, or Companions, of the said Most Honourable Order :—

John Mervion BENN, Permanent Secretary, Ministry of Education for Northern Ireland.
John Francis CLAYTON, Deputy Director of Public Prosecutions.
David DICKSON, H.M. Senior Chief Inspector of Schools, Scottish Education Department.
William Rosecliffe ELLIOTT, Senior Chief Inspector, Department of Education and Science.
Basil GRAY, C.B.E., Keeper of Oriental Antiquities, British Museum.
Philip Arthur HUFTON, Deputy Director (Aircraft), Royal Aircraft Establishment, Farnborough, Ministry of Technology.
Richard Brian Meredith KING, Deputy Secretary, Ministry of Overseas Development.
Professor Sir William Herbert MERRIMAN, D.Sc., Senior Director of Development, General Post Office.
Norman Charles PRICE, Deputy Chairman, Board of Inland Revenue.
Italo de Lisle RADICE, Comptroller General, National Debt Office.
Jack Leslie RAMPTON, Deputy Secretary, Ministry of Power.
Charles Edgar SHERWIN, lately Director of Warship Design, Ministry of Defence.
Reginald Stanley SWIFT, Under Secretary, Department of Health and Social Security.
Henry Moir WILSON, C.M.G., M.B.E., Chief Scientist (Army), Ministry of Defence.

CENTRAL CHANCERY OF THE ORDERS OF KNIGHTHOOD

ST. JAMES'S PALACE, LONDON S.W.1

14th June 1969

The QUEEN has been graciously pleased, on the occasion of the Celebration of Her Majesty's Birthday, to give orders for the following promotions in, and appointments to, the Most Distinguished Order of Saint Michael and Saint George :

C.M.G.

To be Ordinary Members of the Third Class, or Companions of the said Most Distinguished Order :—

Professor Charles Henry DOBINSON. For services to education overseas.
Arthur Stanley George HOARE, lately Managing Director, Commonwealth Development Finance Company Ltd.
Arthur Patrick HOCKADAY, Assistant Under-Secretary of State, Ministry of Defence.
Philip Bicknell RAY, Attached Ministry of Defence.

A 2   Contents list on last page

Announcements about Alastair Panton's OBE and CB awards.
Order of the British Empire medal – column two, tenth name;
Companion of the Order of the Bath – column one, section
four, fifth name.

Recorded in *The Gazette* (*London Gazette*), issue 38797, 2 January 1950 and issue
44863, 14 June 1969.

Map showing Waerschoot in northern Belgium, where Alastair
Panton's plane fell on 14 July 1940. Waerschoot is south-east of
Bruges, about seven miles from Eecloo.

Map kindly sourced and supplied by RAF Hendon.

A NOTE BY
DAVID PANTON

As the David mentioned at the beginning of my father's book, I should like to say how delighted I am that *Six Weeks of Blenheim Summer* is to find a wider audience at last. It does, as my father writes in his own introduction, come from my childhood questions to him about his experiences during the Battle of France, and most of the incidents agree with what he told me during the walks we used to have when he was the CO at Cranwell in Lincolnshire in about 1958.

The horror at what my father saw in France, and later, was also real. It left him with a lifelong aversion to Germans, although he admitted that they saved both his sight – by taking a burned and blinded shot-down pilot to a field hospital – and his life – by taking him prisoner. It was what he saw of their treatment of Russian prisoners of war that stayed with him. In 1957, my primary school organised a trip to see the President of West Germany arrive and travel down The Mall with the Queen, but he banned me from that.

Nevertheless, it was war itself that he really hated, as it took away his much-loved eldest brother and almost all of the friends of his youth. He told me once that only three of the twenty-five members of his Cranwell RAF College year saw, what to him was, the empty victory of 1945. If my father knew his story was being published, I think – in addition to his family – he would wish it to be dedicated to the memory of those who died on the *Lancastria*.

May they, and my greatly admired father, rest in peace.

Cunard liner, the *Lancastria*.

PRISONER OF WAR

Sergeant Stride was burned to death in his turret. I heard him screaming continually as I was trying to land the burning aircraft. I was unable to speak with him over the inter-com. These screams died just as the aircraft crashed, and the turret was a mass of flame when I found myself outside the cockpit lying on the ground.

These are Alastair's words, taken from a Ministry of Defence questionnaire that he, as all prisoners of war were, was required to complete after their captivity ended. The 'burning aircraft' he refers to was the Bristol Blenheim he was flying, from which he managed to escape before it was engulfed in fire. This happened on 14 July 1940.

Grandfather survived the crash, albeit with horrific

injuries including terrible burns to his eyes – he was completely blind for over a week. Soon after he fell, he was captured by Germans and taken to a military hospital. According to his records, he was not transferred from the hospital to his first prisoner of war camp until December of that year.

Grandfather suffered then as many other servicemen suffered that summer, and throughout the war, the physical pain of almost being burned alive; the trauma of hearing someone you are close to experience agony beyond imagination; the fear of the unknown when being taken prisoner; and the sadness of lost freedom. That was how Grandfather's five years as a prisoner of war began.

Sergeant Stride was his wireless operator; his navigator, Sergeant Farrow, managed to escape, and was also taken prisoner.

❧

This chapter is not being written to provide an encyclopaedic account of life as prisoner of war; I am including it to give insight to the reader of what some aspects of captivity may have been like. As well as being a proficient pilot, Grandfather loved to express himself through his writing. He wrote three short stories, all of which I believe are a heartening look back to his time in captivity. These stories are at the end of this chapter, and I hope you will find them as enjoyable as they are informative. I am sure this is what Grandfather intended:

- 'The Boots' is the story of a successful Spitfire fighter pilot's arrival in a PoW camp, and what happens to him as he tries to settle into everyday routine.
- 'The Longest Tunnel in England' examines the respect and trust that might have built between German guards and British prisoners of war.
- 'Meredith' is a story of what it was like to escape and be recaptured.

While they are written in the first person, Grandfather calls himself 'Adrian Blair'. All three stories have been shared before: they were read out on BBC Radio Two in February and July 1968 and in February 1969. As I said, this chapter is not intended to be in any way encyclopaedic, but before reading Grandfather's stories, I hope it is helpful to read a short background to life as a PoW, according to what I have learned about Grandfather's experience, and according to what has been officially documented.

Thank you to the BBC Written Archives Centre for releasing copies of these stories for publication in *Six Weeks of Blenheim Summer*.

Prisoner of war camps sprang up in their thousands during the course of the Second World War throughout Europe, Asia, America, North Africa, Russia and Japan. The experience of each PoW would have varied greatly from camp to camp, but the most decisive factor as to how a PoW was treated was nationality. Russian prisoners, as my Uncle David mentions in his short piece at the end of Grandfather's account, were treated appallingly by the Germans. Thousands died of starvation and diseases such as typhoid and cholera, many were frequently beaten and forced to undertake hard labour, and thousands more were murdered outright – some buried alive, others taken to concentration camps and shot.

This was principally because Russia was not a

signatory of the Geneva Convention on prisoners of war, which was written and signed by forty-seven countries in 1929. The Convention contained a list of articles which stipulated how PoWs were to be treated and, while there were exceptions, the many countries who had signed up to these rules respected them. So, while life for most Allied PoWs was probably dreary and mundane, they did not starve or suffer unduly and had access to limited recreational activity and medical care. That said, not all nationalities were treated equally – British and American PoWs generally received the best treatment, Poles fared the worst, and the Japanese suffered as the Russians did because Japan, too, was not a signatory of the 1929 Convention.

'Escape' activity would have preoccupied the lives and minds of the majority of PoWs. Escaping, almost always by means of tunnelling, was something PoWs were expected to try to do. It was actually stipulated in the 1929 Convention that while prisoners were required to 'observe military discipline and courtesy', they 'could attempt to escape at their own risk' and, if recaptured, escapees should not be punished, although a short period in solitary confinement ('the cooler') could be expected. A few lonely days was a risk most PoWs were prepared to take. Official 'escape committees' were established in the camps and the planning and digging of tunnels, while physically exhausting, was often very well organised and sensibly undertaken.

Escaping, however, was not an activity PoWs attempted simply for its own sake. Military honour and patriotism were also powerful motivators; servicemen through and through, many wanted to regain their status on the battlefield and continue to protect their country.

Grandfather was no exception. I am certain that early on in his captive years – as soon as his physical strength returned – he would have started to plan his escape. In a further official MoD questionnaire, Grandfather was asked if he 'made any attempted or partly successful escapes', to which he replied: 'I was engaged in routine escaping activities until May 1944, when I suddenly lost interest.'

What happened in May 1944, I will never know. It makes me sad to think that perhaps Grandfather had lost hope, or become weak. However, May 1944 was a month before the D-Day landings and even though Grandfather – and other remaining PoWs – would not have been able to predict its success, the fact it was being planned and was imminent may have given Grandfather hope of proper liberation, and so the need to try and escape through PoW-made tunnels would have lessened, if only slightly. This, however, would only have been the case if he knew of the D-Day plan, but, as it had been master-minded for almost a year, it is quite possible that some sort of unofficial intelligence had reached Grandfather and his fellow prisoners. Also of huge significance was the fact that, at this time, Grandfather was being held at *Stalag Luft III* where, only two months earlier, fifty of his colleagues had been shot by the Germans for escap-ing. I expect this put the fear of God into the remaining PoWs, Grandfather included.

Grandfather was incarcerated in four different camps during his five years of captivity, including two stays at *Stalag Luft III*, which was then in Sagan, Germany, but is now in Żagań, Poland (because of the German/Polish border changes that took place shortly after the end of hostilities in 1945). *Stalag Luft III* was the camp to which 'serial escapees' were often sent as it was notoriously difficult to tunnel under, largely because the soil was sandy and the buildings were deliberately raised from the ground.

In spite of the challenges, it was from *Stalag Luft III* that an incredible underground tunnel was dug and, on 24 March 1944, seventy-six servicemen escaped through it. Called 'Harry', and made famous by the film *The Great Escape*, the tunnel languished about 30 feet beneath the surface, was 2 feet wide and some 365 feet long. Sadly, though, the escape ended in tragedy and almost all of the escapees were recaptured. Fifty were executed, on the orders of Hitler, in violation of the 1929 Geneva Convention. Following the escape, the Germans took an inventory of the camp and found out just how extensive the operation had been: 4,000 bed boards had gone missing, as well as the complete disappearance of 90 double bunk-beds, 635 mattresses, 192 bed covers, 161 pillow cases, 52 twenty-man tables, 10 single tables, 34 chairs, 76 benches, 1,212 bed bolsters, 1,370 beading battens, 1,219 knives, 478 spoons, 582 forks, 69 lamps, 246 water cans, 30 shovels, 1,000 feet (300 metres) of electric wire and 600 feet (180 metres) of rope, and 3,424 towels and 1,700 blankets had been used.

Grandfather was imprisoned at the camp at this time, but I do not have any records attaching his name to 'Harry' (either in the planning or in the digging stage), or any indication that he went through it.

However, his escape activities from another Polish camp, *Oflag XXIB*, have been documented.[2]

Alastair was sent to this camp in September 1942, and remained there until April 1943. It was from here that Grandfather assisted with the digging of a tunnel called the 'Asselin Tunnel', under latrines in the camp. At one stage in late 1942 six tunnel projects were underway beneath *Oflag XXIB*, progressing towards the perimeter wire. During this time, Grandfather tunnelled alongside Squadron Leader 'Jimmy' James, who had earlier survived the escape from *Stalag Luft III*, and the subsequent interrogation – under torture – which followed. Grandfather's second stint at *Stalag Luft III* followed *Oflag XXIB*.

Only history knows if Grandfather successfully crawled through any of the tunnels he helped to dig under the dingy latrines used by inmates of *Oflag XXIB*. We will never know for sure. But we can be sure that Grandfather, and his many comrades, spent much of their prisoner of war years underground digging in a bid for freedom. Freedom for himself, freedom for his friends and freedom so, once again, he could fight for his country.

---

2 In Squadron Leader 'Jimmy' James's book *Moonless Night*, first published by William Kimber & Co Ltd in 1983.

Map detailing location of the German prisoner of war camps as they were in 1940–45.

Map kindly sourced and supplied by the Research Department at RAF Hendon.

Personal documents from Alastair Panton's prisoner of war file:
German PoW identification card and the first page from his
Ministry of Defence questionnaire. All PoWs were required to
complete such a document after repatriation.

Documents kindly supplied by the Ministry of Defence.

'THE BOOTS'

This is a prisoner of war story, but it is not about escaping.

Early in 1941 some 500 British officer prisoners of war, the majority from the Royal Air Force, were in a small camp on the flat Baltic plain. The wind was bitterly cold, and there was 2 feet of snow on the ground. I was reading in my room, when the door was flung open with a crash. A new bunch of prisoners from the Luftwaffe interrogation centre was arriving that morning.

'Have your heard? Red Marley's here. Now we'll have some proper news.' The speaker, Mackay, a twenty-year-old fighter pilot, spoke excitedly. 'What's more, he'll stir up some trouble for the Goons. He won't stand for being pushed around.'

Red Marley had become a household name and a

legendary character at the same time in a few short weeks in the Battle of Britain, but now he must have come to grief, and been captured. I had heard a good deal about him, and I looked forward to meeting such a famous fighter pilot. I also wanted to see how he would react to the calamitous shift in his circumstances. I was already aware that reputation was a very fallible guide as to how a person would behave in a prison camp.

I soon met Marley. The Senior British Officer arranged for him to have one of the single rooms in the block I occupied. I was the block member on the escaping committee. I knew the Senior British Officer was briefing him about the general set-up, but what I had to tell him could easily wait until the evening. Early in the afternoon, I was talking to a friend in another block when Mackay searched me out.

'I say, Blair, Wing Commander Marley wants to see you.'

'What, now?' I asked. 'I was going to see him this evening.'

'Yes, now. He particularly said right away.' Mackay was full of importance. The others in the room I was visiting were grinning, and one said, 'I hear His Master's Voice. You'd better run along like a good dog, Adrian.' I went back to my block, knocked on Marley's door, and entered. He was plump, medium height, and red-haired. He looked excited. New-comers often were, particularly the special ones, while they were still a nine-day wonder. Soon they became part of the background, working out their own existence in the drab routine.

'Good afternoon, sir,' I said. 'I'm Blair. You wanted to see me!'

'Certainly I do.' Marley spoke sharply. 'Aren't you the block member on the escaping committee? Why haven't you been to see me sooner? I want the complete gen about the escaping set-up.'

'Well, sir, I thought I'd give you time to settle in. I was coming this evening to tell you what was happening, and to find out if you were interested in taking part.'

'Settle in? Interested? What the hell do you mean? Of course I'm interested. As for settling in, you don't think this place is going to hold me, do you? I tell you, as soon as I've worked something out, my name's Walker. I'm off.'

'Oh, good,' was my feeble comment. I looked out of the window at the heavy snow drifts. 'But it's still damn cold, it would be difficult to get very far even if you did get outside the wire.'

'Cold? Rot!' Give me ten determined men and I'll storm the Goon boxes, take over the camp. Aggressive spirit. That's what you chaps need. Press on. Carry the war to the enemy. Don't let up. Fight! Fight!' His eyes flashing, he was pacing up and down his small room, three paces each way. I listened aghast as a series of clichés poured out, all as impractical as they were milit-ant. I thought he must be acting in part for my benefit. Surely nobody could be ignorant enough to be genuine, in thinking like that. At that moment, as if in ironic applause at this outburst, the sentry in the nearby tower warmed his machine-gun by firing into a bank of snow just outside the wire. I had a sudden vision of Marley and his ten determined men being riddled.

'Pooh,' Marley sneered, looking up at the tower. 'Tell me what's being planned at the moment.' I told him about the tunnel we were working on from our block, scheduled to break in about four months, and of three or four individual schemes for one or two people, which had been registered with the committee. These individual schemes were in abeyance until the weather was warmer. I ended up saying, 'If you'd like to take part in the tunnel, sir, I may be able to find a place on one of the shifts.'

'Yes, all right.' He was off-hand about our tunnel. 'But I won't be here when it breaks, so I'll take part just to help out. There is one thing. I must have some boots. I've only got these at the moment.' He pointed at his flying boots.

'Oh, there's no trouble about footwear.' I was relieved to talk about something practical. 'We've just had a consignment of clothing from the Red Cross, you can have a choice of heavy army ammunition boots, or light RAF boots. There's a clothing officer in the block, and I'll tell him to get you fixed up.'

'Fair enough,' Marley said. 'Tell him to look sharp. I don't want to waste time. I'll see you again in a few days to register my escape plan with you.'

The next evening, Marley appeared at the door of my room where my three room-mates and I were playing bridge. He held out a pair of heavy army boots. 'Here they are! I shall break them in now. Four miles a day to start with round the circuit to soften them up.' We listened politely, suspending our bidding, and offered him a cup of coffee, which he refused, saying he was off, to get on with drawing his maps.

After he had gone, we went on with our bidding without comment. At the end of the hand someone murmured, 'As he softens his boots, he'd better toughen himself. He looks as if he's only used to walking as far as his sports car is parked.'

The circuit was the track around the compound inside the wire, beaten out by prisoners walking round and round. Apart from the cutting wind, walking on it was not very pleasant, because the surface of the hard-packed snow was like glass. The next morning I saw poor Marley (I regret I already thought of the man as 'poor') hobbling painfully round in the stiff heavy boots, slipping about. After fifteen minutes he was limping and gave up.

For the next few days he talked much about aggression and the offensive spirit to anyone who would listen. I asked him to come down on a shift in our tunnel with us. We gave him an easy job on the railway line bringing earth back from the face, but the very cramped space, the stinking air, and the dank earth were a severe shock to him. He held us up badly, and was soon shaking with claustrophobia. The tunneller nearest to him suggested tactfully he'd done enough for the first time, and he was eased out. He never asked, or was asked, to come again.

He tried once more to do 4 miles on the circuit, but the previous day's blisters stopped him after five minutes. He dubbined his boots and said he would wait for the weather to improve.

About a week later he sent for me again. 'Adrian, I haven't quite worked out the final details of my scheme, but I'll let you know soon.'

'Good, sir. By the way, what sort of a scheme are you thinking of? Maybe I can help. Perhaps I can save you going over a lot of ground which has already been covered.' However ingenious an escape plan was, there were only four ways out: over the wire; through the wire; under the wire; and through the gate. Whatever Marley had in mind, if he had anything definite in mind, he'd surely need help of some sort.

'No, I don't need any help, thank you. It's all in here.' He tapped his head. 'I've done a lot of chatting to people and heard their ideas.' There was an evasiveness about Marley which made me fairly sure he did not really have anything in mind. As it turned out, he never registered a scheme at all.

Weeks passed and the snow melted. Marley learned to play bridge, and strangely, perhaps for the first time in his life, he started to read a great deal. The boots lay under his bed, dust now thickly coating the dubbin, only being moved when the orderly's broom hit them.

Our tunnel was ready to break, and out of politeness, as he was the senior officer in our block, I went to his room to ask him if he wanted to go out by it.

'Would you like to draw for a place, sir? I'm afraid the first thirty places are booked for the workers, but you may care to have one of the next ten places.' The chances of even thirty making it were pretty remote, but people liked to be given a chance.

Marley was lying on his bed reading, holding up his book to catch the sunshine which was streaming through his window. He looked at me for a moment and said, 'May I think about it and let you know tomorrow?'

The next morning he took me to one side. 'I thought a lot last night about your tunnel. I am very sorry to say that I must turn your offer down. My wife is not well at home, and it wouldn't be fair on her to add to her anxiety.' How she would ever know anything about the tunnel at all, certainly in time to be anxious about it, he did not say. I did not press him.

The metamorphosis from the fire-eating new arrival was now complete. In his Spitfire Marley was fearless, superbly able. Now, after a few months, he was only another prisoner, ready to help when asked, and kind and considerate to all. He read novels continually and indiscriminately, often three a day. As he lay on his bed, there was a constant whisper of turning pages. He hardly knew what he had read. I once heard someone ask him about a novel he had read that morning.

'Red, what's this book like?'

'Oh, it's excellent, I think...'

'What's it about?'

'Oh, it's about a chap, I think.'

The truth is, of course, escaping wasn't for everybody. It was no good, and quite impractical, for everybody to think they should burst their way out of a prison camp simply because they had been told it was their duty to do so. It was their duty, but only within reason. To be a successful escaper, certain physical and mental attributes were essential. If you were too fat, to excitable, too clumsy or too nervous, if you were too slow-witted or too slow-footed, then you only stood in the way of better-equipped people if you did try to escape. You were much better occupied reading on your bed like Marley, and helping in the hundred and one ways in which your aid was required. Lastly, whatever you were, or whoever you were, before you were captured, was absolutely no guide as to whether you would be a successful escaper. This philosophy became accepted fairly quickly among us, and Marley's boots became a not unkind by-word for lost causes and failed endeavours.

Marley moved from the Baltic coast in due course to the large Luftwaffe prisoner of war camp at Sagan in Silesia, and his boots moved with him. Perhaps he clung to them as a talisman. Perhaps, as long as he had them, he could go on dreaming of some daring escape, of getting back home, of bursting into one of the Shepherd Market pubs, calling out 'I'm back', and listening to cries of delighted wonder from the girls.

Whatever the reason, the boots found their accustomed place under Marley's bed. Early in 1945 the Russian advance into Germany gathered momentum and the Sagan prisoners were given two hours' warning to leave, only taking with them what they could carry. Marley had agonising priorities to determine about cigarettes, books, food and clothes. The boots were left behind.

Well, the war was clearly ending soon, and there was no point in escaping. He could not face the fact that for him there never had been any point in thinking about it. Also he had his own good shoes sent out in a clothing parcel from home.

In late 1945 a friend of mine, an ex-prisoner of war who knew all about Red Marley's boots, was escorted by the Russians to Sagan in connection with an Imperial War Graves Commission matter. The compound which he and Red Marley had once occupied was strangely unchanged. He walked through the huts, his memories and the atmosphere of the weary war years of captivity pressing around him. He passed Red Marley's room, and there, lying under the bed, were the boots.

He picked them up and gave them to the first farm labourer he saw, who was delighted to have them. I like to think the boots, too, were pleased to be needed at last after so many frustrating years.

The first time I saw Grismann was late in 1940. Stiff, cold and extremely grimy, I had stumbled out of the door of a 'Quarante Hommes Huit Chevaux' in which forty-eight of us, Air Force prisoners of war, had been travelling for three days from the Luftwaffe interrogation centre.

A wide ring of armed guards surrounded the siding into which our truck and three others had been shunted. Inside this ring Luftwaffe NCOs and interpreters were trying to form us into some sort of military formation; we were to be marched to the prisoner of war camp, which was 2 miles away across the flat Baltic coast-land of windswept sand. The Germans were being reasonable, good-tempered; we, enjoying the relative freedom from our cramped trucks, were in no hurry to start. Before long, the officer in charge of our reception, an Oberleutnant, began to show signs of impatience. The December evening was drawing in and he wanted to have us safely behind wire before dark. It was then I became aware of Unterofficier Grismann, who had been talking to the Oberleutnant. He saluted, turned from his officer and called out loudly, but calmly, 'Come along, shentlemen, please. Form up for roll-call.'

He spoke English fluently with a not unpleasant guttural undertone. 'Hot showers and a hot meal await you.' A howl of derision arose. Grismann's dark-skinned craggy features broke into a grin which closed his eyes. 'Gentlemen, I promise you. Roast beef, chicken, or some such thing at least.' He turned and strode off down the line, laughing.

I was to know the sight of him all too well in the months and years to come. His appearance was military but blurred at the outlines; his strong legs were slightly bowed; he rolled when he walked; his hat was always, a little, on the back of his head; and his trousers above his scuffed jackboots bagged slightly at the knees and drooped slightly at the seat. He seldom left us, being continually in our compound; if he had no specific task he was often there merely wandering around, looking and listening. There was little he did not know, and he was a constant danger to our clandestine activities because his movements were unpredictable. There were many arguments about him, and the differences of opinion were often violent.

Few things upset him, he shrugged off normal rudeness such as those remarks about the 'The Third and Last Reich', and his good humour was almost tireless. This was a source of irritation to many, and he was also accused, often, of being two-faced; he was (as I have said) always with us, usually jovial and friendly; he would find out something and report it, and another 'scheme' would die. Grismann was doing his duty, and the fact that he did it with humour made him dangerous. It did not, to my mind, make him two-faced.

It was very difficult for prisoners to be objective and it was much in Grismann's favour that he quickly appreciated this, and rarely bore animosity towards those who showed their dislike of him. I came to know him very well early on, when I was given two jobs by the escape committee.

I had to review the organisation in the camp for dealing with 'parcels from home' to see what opportunities there were for smuggling escape material; I also had to 'cultivate' Grismann. The two could be carried out conveniently together since one of Grismann's main tasks was supervision of the parcels store and the distribution to prisoners. We tried to corrupt any German who, through the nature of his duties, we saw often on his own. The process was a gradual one of small beginnings, small bribes and favours, leading to a point when the German was hopelessly compromised; small returns from the German at first, an egg or a cigar, turned into valves and railway passes handed across in terror of exposure. We could afford no scruples.

I soon found out that Grismann was not to be cultivated; he was from the start completely incorruptible, and remained so to the end. The parcels store was outside our compound in one of the headquarters administrative buildings, and, the first day I worked there, I was under Grismann's supervision with another 'parcels officer', Sam Carlton. Sam was a lean, taciturn Canadian.

We were opening parcels, having the contents checked, and doing them up loosely for handing over to the addressee. We stopped work to make a cup of coffee on the coke stove.

'Have a cup of coffee, Grismann?' I asked casually.

'Thank you, Mr Blair. I do not require it.'

'Oh, come on.'

'Thank you, no!'

'Bit of chocolate, then,' Sam said, 'or a cigarette?'

'I do not smoke on duty, gentlemen, thank you, nor do I require chocolate.' Grismann paused and chuckled. 'Whatever your propaganda says, I am very well fed. But don't mind me, you have your refreshment.'

We said no more. Indeed Grismann left no room for manoeuvre, and in addition we were feeling a little silly at the contrast between the stories at home about German shortages and the reality. Grismann knew all about this contrast and he and the others often used it as a basis for jibes. At that time we were often made to look foolish by our propaganda. In all the time I knew him, he never accepted a single cigarette or square of chocolate or cup of tea from any prisoner.

The years passed, and Grismann learned to speak a remarkable flow of RAF idiom. He also became an Oberfeldwebel. Otherwise he was unchanged; he was still cheerful and his trousers still bagged and drooped. Bombing of Germany had now reached serious proportions, but he gave the impression it was not his affair. The Führer could look after that; his home was then too far east for our bombers, and his business was to guard prisoners of war. Except for occasional periods when he was on leave, my connection with him had been continuous for nearly three years, when, late in 1943, it was broken most ignominiously for me.

Early one morning I was coming up from the midnight shift of a tunnel on which I was working, with Sam Carlton immediately behind me. As I pulled myself out of the hatch, I found myself looking into the face of a triumphant security officer and a room full of Germans. What had happened and how they had evaded our well-tried look-out system I could not think. I never did find out because Sam and I were whisked away to the cooler and a few days later removed to another prison camp. I saw nobody who could have told me until after the war, and then I couldn't be bothered to find out.

Together with two soldiers, Grismann was detailed to escort us to our new camp. The journey passed uneventfully. He made us as comfortable as he could, and took no chances of letting us give him the slip. We arrived at a depressed town, in Poland, just after sunset.

The camp was on a hill outside the town, and from the railway station the usual lights round the usual wire looked inexpressibly dreary. It was raining slightly.

'God, what a dump!' Sam muttered, looking up the hill. Grismann heard him.

'Well, Mr Carlton,' he said, smiling, 'you are to blame. We provided a nice camp for you in Silesia and you would try to escape all the time. It is your own fault if you become uncomfortable.'

'Nice camp!' Tired and irritated, Sam exploded. 'Don't talk such tripe, Grismann. What do you think it matters what the camp is like? They are all lousy, and even if they weren't, they are still prisons. We're still cooped up in them.'

There was a long silence while Grismann looked at us both in turn. The two guards looked shocked; while they could not understand English, there was no mistaking the tone the usually quiet Sam used to their Oberfeldwebel. I wondered for a moment whether Grismann was going to turn nasty, but I should have known better.

'Forgive me, Mr Carlton.' He was now unsmiling. 'That was stupid of me. Believe me, I think I do understand how you feel.'

Sam was immediately contrite. 'I'm sorry I blew up. Thank you for looking after us on this journey as you have done. I'm glad you were in charge of our escort.'

'Don't mention it.' Grismann was suddenly, surprisingly, gruff. 'I'm sorry that you are leaving us. That is all I meant to say.' He paused and looked at the prison camp on the skyline. 'I'm sorry this has to be. This is not, I think, a good camp at all. It is run by the Wehrmacht.'

He did not speak again, and the bluff, leg-pulling man I knew so well had gone. At the camp shortly afterwards, he went through the formalities of handing us over quickly, without looking at us. He then said, 'Goodbye, Mr Blair. Goodbye, Mr Carlton,' turned and was gone. With a shock of realisation, I understood; Grismann liked us. Although we had utterly failed in 'cultivating' him, neither Sam or I had ever been rude to him, nor had we never made a fool of him. If ever we had outwitted him personally, he accepted this without rancour. Lastly, he was sorry for us, although I think it is true to say that we weren't (at any rate for long) sorry for ourselves.

For the rest of the war, the prisoners I was with had never been with Grismann, and I heard no more of him. Towards the end, for two nights, the news mentioned that Grismann's home town was being attacked by Bomber Command just in front of the advancing Red Army, and I wondered if Grismann's family were still there. In 1943 it had seemed so safe. After I returned home I met in the Royal Air Force Club another ex-prisoner who had been with Grismann to the end. In casual conversation I was told that Grismann's family had all been killed. What had happened to Grismann himself no one knew. Just before their camp had been over-run by the First Armoured Division, Grismann had gone off with a small armed party to join a hastily formed Home Guard unit.

In the spring of 1946 I had a long weekend off from the flying training station where I was being converted to jet aircraft. Everything I did was still exciting; the flying frankly thrilled me; and I appreciated small things – hot water and well-cut clean clothes particularly – enormously. One way and another, as I walked down the long platform at Waterloo to board the Salisbury train, my spirits matched the April sunshine. The sight of a number of German prisoners of war crowded into a train on the other side of the platform hardly penetrated my consciousness or my complacency. I was nearing the end of the prisoners' train when I heard my name being called.

I spun around, and there, leaning out of a carriage, a grin splitting his face from ear to ear, was Grismann.

'Grismann!' I hurried to his carriage. 'I can't believe it. I am glad to see you.' And I was.

'Are you all right? Is there anything I can give you?' I started to feel in my tunic pockets.

'I don't need anything, Mr Blair, thank you.' His attitude to favours and presents had not changed. 'You know how it is. I only want to return home.'

I hesitated. 'Any – any news of your family?'

'They are by a miracle safe in the US Zone.'

'I'm so glad. I heard your home had been bombed, and I feared for you.'

Whistles blew, flags waved, and Grismann's train began to move. I followed it down the platform beside him, but the train began to pull away from me. I asked, inadequately, 'What are you doing with yourself?'

Grismann suddenly adopted a clownish expression of extreme craft and furtiveness. 'Shhh! Don't talk so loudly!'

The train gathered speed thunderously.

'Don't tell anyone,' he yelled, waving and grinning, 'but I'm building the Longest Tunnel in England.'

'MEREDITH'

I found myself in many improbable circumstances as a prisoner of war, and wandering round the marshalling yards at Hamburg at night with Sam Carlton, looking for a goods truck with 'Switzerland' written on it, was one of them.

Sam was a Canadian, and he and I had been together ever since we went through the Luftwaffe interrogation centre at the end of 1940. He had the most wonderful night vision.

A feeling of unreality had been with us for some days, ever since we had left the Rukow escape tunnel. We were out, free for the first time, and the change and excitement after so much dullness was intoxicating. From Rukow we had walked for sixty-odd miles to Schweinfurt with only the shortest possible stops, anxious to be as far away as possible from the camp, and the other escapers, as the uproar broke out, which it was bound to when our break was revealed. As we intended, we had taken a train for Berlin from Schweinfurt, the terminus of the German-gauge railways. We had travelled to Berlin, where we changed our cover stories and identities.

We were now Danish dental mechanics, ostensibly heading for Freiburg, near the Swiss border, and we had chosen this route because we would be unlikely to meet a policeman who could speak Danish, or who knew anything about dental machinery.

Without any trouble or discomfort we had crossed Berlin and caught a train to Hamburg. Unfortunately, this orderly method of progress had to stop, because we had run out of German money for more railway tickets. One of the snags of a big tunnel break was that the escape committee's resources had to be shared among a large number, and our Reichsmarks only lasted as far as Hamburg. From there onwards, if we were to reach anywhere near Switzerland, we did so on our own resources. Confident after the ease and smoothness of our journey so far, we were looking for a suitable wagon to stow away in, only faintly aware that we were being highly optimistic.

We were beginners; so much of our attention and energies had been concentrated on digging the tunnel that we hadn't planned our journey in detail. Our general intention was to cross into Switzerland, but how we got there once our money ran out, we had left to chance. But, already we had exceeded our expectations. We had imagined so many snags, none had occurred, and now anything seemed possible. Only once, at Schweinfurt two days earlier, had we been completely taken aback.

With our third-class tickets we were seated in the train with about ten minutes to go, alone in our carriage. We were delighted with ourselves at having, as we thought, got clear away from the pursuit and our fellow prisoners. We were quietly reading daily papers, for colour, when an urgent whisper into the open window between us started us horribly.

'Why aren't you travelling first-class? I am.'

We looked up at the grinning face of Dick Crondall, who was travelling as a consumptive professor, going to Bavaria for a cure. His face had been burned when he was shot down, and he had managed to make himself look pretty ill behind his dark glasses. Nothing was further from the truth; he was wiry, and fit.

'Dick! For God's sake!' Sam gasped.

'It's all right. There's no one anywhere near us. I saw you some minutes ago and have been scouting around. You must have made it here pretty quickly. I'm shagged out. Aren't you? I want the train to start so I can have a sleep.'

'We're pretty short of money,' I said. 'How on earth did you scrounge enough to go first-class?'

Dick smirked. 'Well, Adrian, you know I'm a sick professor. You can't expect me to travel hard, can you?'

'What a racketeer you are! Just because you were on the committee you swiped lots of the cash.'

'Racketeer? Me?' Dick looked round. 'Shhh! There's someone coming down the train looking for a seat. I'm off! Good luck!' He adopted a melancholic air, and shuffled off on his stick, coughing thinly. I never saw him again.

That had been nearly three days before. Now in the Hamburg marshalling yard, we continued with our search. Scattered about were top-shaded lamps on high posts; and in the dim, reflected light from these, we found wagons for Russia, the Netherlands, France and Denmark – but nothing for Switzerland.

We crept stealthily about, but we seemed to have the place to ourselves.

'What a cavort,' Sam muttered. 'Cavort', used to imply absurd and uncertain movement, was a word he had picked up from a South African friend of ours, who had also escaped from our tunnel. He had headed for Bavaria, travelling as a Flemish seed and bulb salesman. Later, Sam said, 'I wonder where that crook Dick is.'

'Perhaps some kind German has put him into a hospital,' I answered, and we chuckled at the thought of Dick trying to talk his way past some old Nordic ward-sister. In fact, I discovered later that he had vanished into the Third Reich; and in the years to come I was often to find myself thinking, with a lump in my throat, of our last sight of him, shuffling consumptively down the Schweinfurt platform. It was, indeed, funny at the time; but then, light-hearted as most of our escape activity was, tragedy was never very far away. I suppose we did not really appreciate this, at least until later.

After two hours or so, against all probability, but matching the strangeness of the whole journey, we found a tarpaulin-covered truck, labelled 'Freiburg'.

Through a grill in the side we could see cylindrical bundles wrapped in thick paper which yielded slightly to prodding.

'They're probably bales of cloth.'

'We'd be snug as hell in there.'

'It's an answer to a Kriege's prayer.'

We whispered excitedly together, already in our imaginations rumbling steadily, comfortably, towards freedom – not considering how long the truck was likely to wait in the yard, or how we were to eat and drink on the journey, once we had finished our already small supplies.

'Let's look for a way to get in.'

'It won't be easy. We'll have to close the cover from inside, so that nothing shows outside.'

Side by side, we had just started to work our way round the truck, testing the ropes holding down the tarpaulin, when air raid warnings sounded. Out went the overhead lighting, and a few police whistles sounded. Uncertain, we slipped underneath our truck, and lay peering out into the darkness, chins on the rail, waiting. After a while, anti-aircraft guns erupted very nearby – shredding the silence – and vibration shook dust from the truck onto us.

'The duty Wellingtons are going over,' Sam whispered, 'I wish they would leave us alone.'

'For once you see eye to eye with a few million Goons,' I said, and then felt him stiffen, pressing my arm.

'Down! Still!' I felt rather than saw him lower his head, and hide his face under the inside of the rail, and copied him. Measured, slow footsteps became louder, someone crunched within a yard of us, and passed a short distance away. All our senses were in our ears as we heard him turn on the cindery surface, slithering, and plod past us again. This sequence was repeated, and we realised that we were lying near the end of that someone's beat. I remembered, once, hearing two RAF sergeants talking; they had been in a marshalling yard in an air raid. I inched my mouth to Sam's ear.

'In an air raid, the lights go out and railway police patrol between the lines instead. We'll have to stay put until the all-clear.' And that is what we did, stiffening as our policeman neared, relaxing as his footsteps died, until eventually the all-clear sounded. On came the lights. Another policeman joined our one, and, chattering, they disappeared. After a time, as far as we could tell, we were alone. The patrols seemed to have gone, and the only sounds were the clanks of distant shunting. We came out from under the truck, shaking the dust from our heads, cold and stiff in the keen spring night air.

'We'd better get into this wagon while we can,' said Sam softly; but before I could answer we heard a rustle from between two trucks on the next line. We froze against our truck, feeling horribly exposed. A wary head poked slowly out, and a worried voice whispered, 'I say, Meredith, is that you?'

Sam recovered instantly, and said, using the exaggerated drawl of a Canadian aping an Englishman, 'Sorry, old chap. No!' The head whipped back, and we heard its body leaving smartly.

'Who the hell was that?' I tittered in relief.

'Some escaped Pongo, I should think, by the sound of his voice. Presumably looking for his lost pal Meredith. How clueless can you get?' We continued working our way round the truck, looking for an opening, laughing in whispers together, imagining the marshalling yard to be the scene of a large-scale game of cops and robbers, with assorted Allied prisoners of war in the role of the hunted. As we examined the truck we were constantly looking round, and in doing so I saw two policemen appear at the end of our line of trucks. I pulled Sam round the corner. The police, who were smoking, did not see us, but one was holding a police-dog on a lead, and the dog, sensing our presence, barked sharply.

Immediately we bolted, running on the far side of the trucks from the policemen and dodging into the next row, most unpleasantly aware of the dog and its fangs. Pandemonium broke out; the dog was barking madly, and was answered by other dogs; whistles blew, guttural cries were answered in all quarters, and even a shot rang out; a bell began to toll. We stopped, momentarily, panting, having dodged our immediate pursuers, when from the end of a nearby truck, the unbelievable furtive head appeared again.

'Meredith, is that you?' It was my turn now.

'No! Sorry again!' I called over my shoulder as we spurted off. This repetition was so farcical, that I found myself wanting to give up. How could one try to be a serious escaper with this sort of nonsense going on? There were shouts and running footsteps all round us by now, and when I tripped over the inevitable signal wire, winding myself, I was grabbed before I could get up. When I could breathe reasonably, two policemen marched me off.

'Prisoner of war?'

'Yes.'

'Escaping?'

'Yes.'

'Bad luck.' They chuckled, delighted at their capture. As my excitement and nervous energy wore off, I began to feel very tired. We reached a police station. A cell door was opened to show two beds. Hard as they undoubtedly were, they looked most inviting. I kicked off my shoes and flopped back onto one of them. Tomorrow could look after itself.

As my eyes were closing, I heard Sam's angry voice in the passage. 'I insist on a cell to myself.' I smiled; Sam was giving his familiar, to me, demonstration of not giving a damn for anyone. The cell door opened. Sam saw me, stopped resisting the two policemen who held him, and was shoved in.

'Hullo, Adrian. Tough luck.'

'What happened to you?' I said.

'Shortly after you fell over I ran into six Goons at once and was grabbed.' He sat down on his bed and began to undo his laces. 'You know, they told me that the two with the dog who found us were off duty, taking a short cut home. God, I'm tired. I hope they let us sleep for a bit.'

Outside our cell door the sentry's footsteps stopped. There was a faint click as he opened the flap over the Judas hole, and squinted in. We did not look up. After a few moments, he left. Sam flopped back on his bed, looking up at the ceiling.

'Adrian?'

'Yes?'

'I wonder what happened to those Pongoes.'

'Meredith and his pal?'

'Yes.'

'God knows. They will be very lucky if they weren't caught. The place was crawling with Goons.'

We slept.

I went to an investiture at Buckingham Palace towards the end of 1945. The King was working through a large batch of awards that day and I, with many others, had to wait some time in the fuel-rationed chill of one of the ante-rooms. Some of the bomb-shattered window-panes had not yet been repaired. I met someone who had been at school with me. We chatted, and I learned he had spent the war in the Pacific. I spoke to him about Germany.

After the investiture was over, I saw him again in the courtyard.

'Oh,' he said. 'I've just been talking to an Army officer who was getting an MC for escaping from Germany. I wonder if you knew him?'

'What was his name?'

'Meredith.'

Alastair Panton (right) in a photograph taken at *Stalag Luft*, Barth, in the winter of 1941.

Photograph kindly lent by Andrew Panton.

AUTHOR ENDNOTE

Finally, this part of the book would not be complete without reference to the 'Long March': the journey that thousands of prisoners of war were forced to endure in the closing months of World War Two.

The march marked the beginning of the end of the war, when during the winter of 1944–5 the approach of the Red Army westwards presented the Germans with a major problem: how to deal with the hundreds of PoWs still languishing in camps throughout Germany and the occupied territories. Germany's response was simply to release them, hence the start of what has become known as the 'Long March'. It was horrendous. Prison gates were opened, and hundreds of prisoners were told to leave, totally unprepared for the journey ahead. They walked for around three months in wretched, freezing conditions with little food, water, accommodation or clothes. The march has been described as an agonisingly cold 'shuffle', culminating in Berlin where the former prisoners were held before finally being flown home.

According to his papers, Grandfather was imprisoned at *Stalag Luft III* when the exodus of PoWs began. He may have begun the march but, in February 1945, he was transferred to his final camp, *Stalag III A* in Luckenwalde in Germany, where PoWs were not liberated by the Russians until April.

Pilot Officer Henry Stockings, now ninety-seven years old, is a veteran of the march. I went to see him in his home in Norfolk, and he told me how he and his comrades survived the cold at night by lying close to each other, not in beds, but on the hard floor of factories and warehouses, avoiding rats where possible. He recalled how they ate potato peelings and how many marchers became ill once, after eating copious amounts of raw rhubarb.

Stockings flew Handley Page Hampden bombers as a member of 44 Squadron. With three crew members, he was flying his plane, X2918, towards Cologne as part of a group of nineteen Hampdens on 10 March 1941, when he was shot down near

Venlo in Holland. He managed to survive by landing in a tree, also saving the lives of his crew, E. G. M. Bond, E. W. Dunking and R. J. N. Hanslip. Only two months earlier, Stockings had been awarded the DFC for flying his Hampden, constantly for twelve hours, to Danzig in Poland – the longest flight ever recorded for this type of plane at the time.

Henry Stockings saw many overcome by the physical exhaustion they had to endure during their journey and, as was the case for Grandfather, the most difficult memories have not left him.

Photograph of Pilot Officer Henry Stockings, circa 1940.

Photograph kindly lent by Pauline Bugg.

THE BLENHEIM SOCIETY

'He's bought it' is a phrase that is sadly all too familiar to the 'Blenheim Boys' that are still with us today. Squadron Leader Stanley Dixon, now ninety-three years old, is one of those Boys. He was a sergeant navigator on Blenheims, attached to 254 Squadron during World War Two in 1940–41 and operated over the Low Countries and Norway mainly from Bircham Newton (in Norfolk), Lossiemouth and Shetland. He told me how sometimes his colleagues would just disappear. 'He's bought it' was a gentle way of declaring someone had been killed.

The Bristol Blenheim was operational between 1937 and 1944, and was one of the first British aircraft to have all-metal stressed-skin construction, retractable landing gear flaps, a powered gun turret, and variable-pitch propellers. However, it did not prove to be a match against the German fighters, most notably the Messerschmitt

ALASTAIR PANTON & VICTORIA PANTON BACON

109s, which dominated so forcefully particularly in the early 1940s. Hundreds of men were lost in Blenheims during these wartime years. Some were shot while airborne, others baled out in parachutes (landing safely), and the rest died in explosions on crash-landing.

Given the scale of loss, it could be said that the Blenheim's history is a tragic history. Yet in spite of so many losses, the RAF kept up the fight (in Blenheims and other aircraft) and, together with the rest of the armed forces, were not ultimately defeated.

Germany invaded Norway first, on 9 April 1940, and soon after Britain and France came to Norway's aid with an expeditionary force, including Stanley Dixon. Stan Dixon considered himself to be 'lucky' in that he was part of a crew who flew their Mark IV Fighter Blenheims in Shetland and Norway in this period – away from the intense theatre of the Battle of France, and in a Blenheim armed with Browning machine guns, rather than bombs.

The Allies put up a valiant fight but, by 10 June, Norway had capitulated. This campaign, like the Battle of France, cost the Allies dearly, in both men and equipment. Stan Dixon recalled one of the worst weeks when, in June 1940, eight Blenheims in his squadron were lost over a seven-day period.

250

It is no surprise for me to have learned, directly from Stan Dixon, about the comfort he has drawn in the years since the Second World War from other surviving Blenheim Boys, brought together by the Blenheim Society. It is a wonderful tribute to them, to those who died in Blenheims, and to the aeroplane itself, that a society has been set up to treasure these memories. Stan spoke fondly of his years on Blenheims and of his gratitude to the skill of his pilot, Sergeant Charles Rose, with whom he entrusted his life. While Dixon survived the war, sadly his pilot and friend Rose, by this point a wing commander, did not: he died in 1944 while flying a Mosquito on an anti-shipping raid.

The Blenheim will, I hope, keep its place in history as one of the Second World War's feistiest and most useful of small planes. One of the greatest advantages it had over other aircraft was its range: it could, and did, penetrate deep into enemy territory. In a German night-raid in London on 18 June 1941, Blenheims accounted for five German bombers; more successes came and, later that year, it proved to be the backbone of Fighter Command's night fighter role, used by both Bomber and Fighter Commands. However, in spite of its strengths, the extent of casualties suffered in 1940 couldn't be ignored and the Blenheim was replaced on European frontlines by the more powerful, better-armed and faster Bristol Beaufighter, and the de Havilland Mosquito. In the latter years of the war, the Blenheim's main function was a training aircraft, but it also had its place as a fighter and bomber in battle zones in the Far and Middle East.

The Blenheim Society was officially inaugurated in 1987 and, since then, newsletters have been sent out three times a year to its 650 or so members, recording many of the Boys' memories, and publishing book reviews and, inevitably, obituaries, touchingly written by proud family members. There is no better way to learn about what it was like for the Blenheim Boys during the war years than to read these colourful obits. They are shocking, lively and enriching all at the same time.

The society is also supporting a very exciting Blenheim project currently underway at the Imperial War Museum in Duxford. The Aircraft Restoration Company is busily rebuilding a Bristol Blenheim. At the time of writing (April 2014) much progress has been made, and there is a realistic expectation that it will take to the skies later this year.

If you would like to know more about the Blenheim Society, or the restoration project, the following websites will tell you all you need to know:

www.blenheimsociety.org.uk
www.arc-duxford.co.uk/restorations/blenheim

Sergeants Stanley Dixon and Charles Rose, Lossiemouth, 1940.

Photograph kindly lent by Stanley Dixon.

Air Commodore Alastair Panton DFC OBE CB, circa 1980.

Private Collection.

254

A PROUD AND SHARP DELIGHT

I love to fly from night to day,
And, pendant, wait the first smudged ray
With tired eyes. Then day breaks free;
The cold sky glows; and suddenly
The coastline smiles upon the sea.
And there's no proud and sharp delight
To match the loneliness of flight
Above the clouds. Then, later, high
Over the sunset, I hush the sky
With gliding turns, until I fly
Along the darkening rolling grass
To let my wheels oil-cushioned, pass
Unfaltering from gentle flight,
As gentle as the glimmering light.

Alastair Panton

ACKNOWLEDGEMENTS

While *Six Weeks of Blenheim Summer* tells the story of the Battle of France, I chose to add in the prisoner of war chapter because I simply don't think these years should be forgotten and, by all accounts, Grandfather was as courageous a PoW as he was a pilot. Like many other prisoners, I believe Grandfather would have spent much of his time in captivity planning his escape by digging, with a steely determination, to reach the perimeter wire.

The light at the end of Grandfather's tunnel was freedom, and my first thank-you is to him. I was thirty years old when he died. When I was growing up, I was aware that he'd been very brave in the war, but I had no detailed knowledge of what he actually did. He was just Grandfather – kind, funny, clever but rather quiet and very thoughtful. Of course, I now know so much

ALASTAIR PANTON & VICTORIA PANTON BACON

more and I am so thankful that he took the trouble to record his memories. He says in his own Introduction, 'I hope the family find my record interesting.' We do!

Delving into his past and this part of World War Two has involved lots of digging too. The light at the end of my 'tunnel' is that Grandfather's story will be shared, so that the sacrifice he, and so many others, made will not have been in vain. My second thank-you is to Sam Carter for reading Grandfather's story and giving me the encouragement and backing I needed to take this project forward.

Research is about digging; in this case, digging for information, asking questions, chasing for answers, looking through books, hunting for photographs, sourcing maps. Writing is about searching for words, and placing them on the page over and over again until they seem to be in something like the right order.

I am so grateful to all those who have helped me through my metaphorical tunnel, and enabled me to take Grandfather's story beyond the 'perimeter wire'. In no particular order, my thanks go to:

Henry Stockings and Stanley Dixon for telling me their stories;

Lord Guthrie for his Foreword;

Louis de Bernières, Lord Dannatt, Matthew Parris, Duncan Slater and Brigadier Hugh Monro for their endorsements;

Military historian Andrew Bird for his invaluable help in writing the Prologue;

John Constable-Reeve for the painting of the Blenheim on the jacket of the book, beautifully done in Grandfather's squadron colours – 53 Squadron – with the serial number on it of his plane that fell on 14 July 1940;

Huby and Josie Fairhead at the Norfolk and Suffolk Aviation Museum; your support and kindness is amazing, and our family visits to the museum are always memorable and happy;

The staff in the research library at RAF Hendon, particularly Gordon Leith for all the maps, and Andrew Cormack, Keeper of Visual Arts, Medals and Uniforms for his help with finding information about Alastair's medals, and also for displaying my father's model aeroplanes;

The Blenheim Society: Ian Carter, John Smith, Andrew Pierce, Ron Scott, Tony Lowe and the late Graham Warner. The Society is a wonderful, living memorial to the Bristol Blenheim aeroplane; I wish the Society and the team at Duxford every success with the Blenheim restoration project;

Mike Rigby, who has pointed me in the right direction with lots of research and has been very helpful with scanning documents and taking photographs;

The Imperial War Museum in Lambeth for their help with photographs, particularly Sally Webb and Helen Mavin;

Anna Soubry MP, The Lord Astor of Hever and Paul Stevenson at the MoD for their help in tracking down files;

Claire Catherall in the House of Commons Library;

Tracey Allen, Editor of RAF News and Louise Pullen of RAFA Trade (the publishing and trading company of the RAF Association, RAFA);

Elise Delnatte of the Brussels Air Museum;

Chloe Lamb, Becca Cooper, Pauline Bugg and Kerry Mark for their support;

The National Archives in Kew;

The Biteback team, who have been encouraging from the word go, and most enjoyable to work with! James Stephens, Olivia Beattie, Melissa Bond, Katy Scholes, Suzanne Sangster and Namkwan Cho for the front cover design;

And finally last, but certainly not least, my family:

My uncles Andrew and David Panton. I simply could not, and would not, have brought their father's story to light without their support;

Cousin Julian Panton;

My twin sister Sarah, her husband Christopher and their children Barnaby, Sapphire and Pollyanna; thank you for your excitement about the book and for believing in my ability to finish it; and

Richard, my husband, and my darling boys Rollo and Ranulph. Rollo is seven years old as this is being written, and he would be the first to admit he's obsessed with aeroplanes, and learning about World War Two. Ranulph is only four, but equally happy with a toy aeroplane in his hand. Thank you, to all my 'R's; and

Also thank you to Queenie, my sister's dog, and my very own Jack Russell, Zephyr. Her walks have been a bit short over the past few weeks but she hasn't complained!

Victoria Panton Bacon
May 2014